MYSTERIES
OF THE
MESSIAH

UNVEILING DIVINE CONNECTIONS FROM GENESIS TO TODAY

STUDY GUIDE + STREAMING VIDEO
SIX SESSIONS

RABBI JASON SOBEL

WITH WAYNE HASTINGS

HarperChristian
Resources

Mysteries of the Messiah Study Guide
© 2021 by Rabbi Jason Sobel

Requests for information should be addressed to:
HarperChristian Resources, 3900 Sparks Dr. Se, Grand Rapids, Michigan 49546

ISBN 978-0-310-14702-2 (softcover)
ISBN 978-0-310-14703-9 (ebook)

All Scripture quotations, unless otherwise indicated, are from the Tree of Life (TLV) Translation of the Bible. Copyright © 2015 by The Messianic Jewish Family Bible Society.

Scripture marked MSG taken from THE MESSAGE, copyright © 1993, 2002, 2018 by Eugene H. Peterson. Used by permission of NavPress. All rights reserved. Represented by Tyndale House Publishers, Inc.

Any internet addresses (websites, blogs, etc.) and telephone numbers in this study guide are offered as a resource. They are not intended in any way to be or imply an endorsement by HarperChristian Resources, nor does HarperChristian Resources vouch for the content of these sites and numbers for the life of this study guide.

HarperChristian Resources titles may be purchased in bulk for church, business, fundraising, or ministry use. For information, please e-mail ResourceSpecialist@ ChurchSource.com.

First Printing February 2021 / Printed in the United States of America

CONTENTS

HOW TO USE THIS GUIDE

The Bible is one of my favorite mystery books. From the opening words of Genesis to the final chapter of Revelation, God's Word is filled with tantalizing clues, fascinating revelations, and an extraordinary plot. Many of the Bible's mysteries have nagged at our imaginations for centuries. There are odd characters, dysfunctional families, bloody battles, and courageous heroes, yet we find incredible wisdom within the writings. And readers ask, "Who is this mystifying protagonist called the Messiah—the Redeemer who will come to save the world?"

During the next six weeks, you and your group will investigate several mysteries that surround Jesus the Messiah. You will dig into Scripture and uncover the connections between the Old and New Testament prophecies that are essential to investigating these mysteries. As Jesus said, "Every *Torah* scholar discipled for the kingdom of heaven is like the master of a household who brings out of his treasure both new things and old" (Mathew 13:52). Each session will spark these connections between the old and new, resulting in an unraveling revelation that will cause your heart to burn with increased hope and overflow with blessing.

The Mysteries of the Messiah video study is designed to be experienced in a group setting (such as a Bible study, Sunday school class, or other small-group gathering) and also as an individual study. Each session begins with a brief welcome section and opening starter questions to get you thinking about the topic. You will then watch a video teaching and jump into some directed discussion questions. You will close each session with a time of prayer.

If you are doing this study with others, each person should have his or her own study guide, which includes video teaching notes, discussion questions, and between-sessions personal studies to help you reflect on the material during the week. You are also encouraged to have a copy of *The Mysteries of the Messiah* book, as reading it alongside the study will provide you with deeper insights and make the journey more complete and meaningful. In addition, the book has many more mysteries and teaching could not be covered in the sessions.

Before you start your adventure, there are a few things to keep in mind that will help you on your journey. First, if you are doing this study with others, the real growth will happen during your small-group time. You will have the opportunity to listen to the weekly teaching and learn from others as each person shares what God is doing in his or her life. To this end, it's important for you to attend each session, as your commitment will build trust among your other group members. If you choose to only "go through the motions," or if you refrain from participating, there is a lesser chance you will find what you're looking for during this study.

Second, small groups can offer a unique opportunity for sharing, learning, and building friendships. So I encourage you to make your small group a safe place where people feel free to share their insights, prayer requests, and even differing opinions. Each person should be able to contribute freely without the stress of judgment or criticism. One way to foster this openness is to not attempt to "fix" people's issues, or theology, but listen and discuss. You want to create a sense of deep community and spiritual growth.

Third, each session contains teaching related to Hebrew and Greek "by the numbers." Most of the world's languages separate numbers from letters, but not Hebrew and Greek. Both languages use letters—their respective alphabets—for numbers. Each letter in the Hebrew and Greek alphabets has a numeric value. Because of this, numbers can spell words and words can add up to numeric values. Numbers are a significant part of uncovering the mysteries of the Messiah, connecting the Testaments, and going deeper in your study of the Bible.

Fourth, this study references several sources from many centuries of Jewish thought. These sources will help you open up the Jewish meaning of many passages and their connection to the Messiah and New Testament. Just as Christian pastors and teachers use multiple sources to explain Scripture, we are bringing together essential sources to study the Messiah.

Finally, most of the Scripture references in this study are from the Tree of Life Version of the Bible. The Tree of Life Version speaks with a decidedly Jewish-friendly voice—a voice like many

Hebrew Alphanumeric Chart

Letter	Name	Value	Letter	Name	Value
א	Aleph	1	ל	Lamed	30
ב	Bet	2	מ	Mem	40
ג	Gimel	3	נ	Num	50
ד	Dalet	4	ס	Samekh	60
ה	Hei	5	ע	Ayin	70
ו	Vav	6	פ	Peh	80
ז	Zayin	7	צ	Tsadee	90
ח	Cheit	8	ק	Qof	100
ט	Tet	9	ר	Resh	200
י	Yod	10	ש	Shin	300
כ	Kaf	20	ת	Tav	400

of the Bible's authors themselves—to recover the authentic context of the Scriptures and biblical faith. It was produced by messianic Jewish and Christian scholars who sought to highlight the rich Hebrew roots of the Christian faith. Since this translation restores the Jewish order and numbering of the books of the Old Testament, you may find that certain verse citations are one number off compared to other translations of the Bible.

Maximum benefits for this study will come from not only commitment to your group but also your own personal study time. The individual study suggestions are there to help guide you deeper into Scripture and enhance your learning. If you miss a personal session, please don't feel you should also skip the group time. Your group is first priority, and you will still be wanted and welcome even if you haven't completed your personal work at home.

It's my hope that *Mysteries of the Messiah* will bring you insights about the Redeemer and how he can be discovered in the many connections throughout the Old and New Testaments. It's my earnest prayer that the uncovering of these mysteries will give you eye-opening moments and new ways to reflect on your life and the Messiah who came to die for you, live again for you, and give you incredible hope for a future with him.

Baruch HaShem! Praise God!

Note: *If you are a group leader, there are additional resources provided in the back of this guide to help you lead your group members in this study.*

FINDING JESUS IN THE STORY OF CREATION

The entire Old Testament points to the coming of the Messiah in the New Testament. We find this from the very first letter and word in Genesis, which reveals that Creation itself was made through the Messiah—that he was the agent of Creation. The story of the Creation sets the foundation of the much larger story that will be revealed in Scripture, which focuses on relationship, redemption, and restoration.

WELCOME

The two disciples trudged down the road to Emmaus. The past few days had been a whirlwind of activity. It had begun when Jesus, whom they believed was the Messiah, had triumphantly entered into Jerusalem and been hailed by the crowds. But this had been quickly followed by Jesus' arrest and several trials before the Jewish and Roman authorities. Near the end of the week, he had been sentenced to death and led away to be crucified. But now, stories were circulating that Jesus' tomb was empty—that he had *risen* from the grave.

It is little wonder the two men were talking about "all the things that had been happening" as they walked (Luke 24:14). But then something unexpected happened. Jesus *himself* came up and starting walking along with them, though they were kept from recognizing him. Jesus could see they were sad and asked what they had been discussing. They recounted all the horror and disappointments they had experienced in the recent days, noting that they had hoped Jesus "was the One about to redeem Israel" (verse 21). They ended with the report they had just received about his tomb being empty and several women seeing a vision of angels.

Jesus replied, "Oh foolish ones, so slow of heart to put your trust in all that the prophets spoke!" (verse 26). He then spoke from the Scriptures to these men, tracking through the Old Testament prophecies to reveal what they said about the Messiah. He taught them the cohesive message of both Testaments, and *"then their eyes were opened and they recognized Him,* and He disappeared from them" (Luke 24:31, emphasis added).

Like these men, my life has been radically transformed as I have delved into the divine connections that reveal the mysteries of the Messiah. And I have seen the lives of many others change as they have learned how the Old and New Testaments connect. When you come to understand the Jewish roots of your faith, you begin to see Jesus' life and ministry from a different perspective. It is like putting on a pair of glasses and seeing things clearly for the first time—all the richness, sharpness, and clarity of details that you might have otherwise missed.

In this study, it is my hope that you, like those disciples on the road to Emmaus, will come to see the Old Testament story in a new way. It is my hope that your eyes will be opened as you learn how the Jewish *roots* and Gentile *shoots* connect. And it is my hope that this exploration of the mysteries of the Messiah will ignite a new love for Jesus and passion for the Bible that will bring you greater hope and transformation in your life.

SHARE

If you or any of your group members are just getting to know one another, take a few minutes to introduce yourselves. Before you watch the video teaching, pair up with another member (perhaps someone you don't know that well) and briefly discuss the following questions:

- What has been your experience studying the Bible? In which part of the Bible have you spent the most time?

- Do you have a favorite Old Testament character? Why is he or she your favorite?

WATCH

Watch the video for session one. (Play the DVD or see the instructions on the inside front cover on how to access the sessions through streaming.) As you watch, use the following outline to record any thoughts or concepts that stand out to you.

The Bible comes alive in amazing ways when we understand how Jesus is in every detail of the Scripture—in both the New Testament *and* the Old Testament.

The first letter in the book of Genesis is the Hebrew letter B, *bet*, found in the word "beginning." The last letter of the book of Revelation is the word "amen," which ends with the Hebrew letter *nun*. The first letter and last letter in the Bible spell the Hebrew word *BeN,* which means "Son." From beginning to the end, the Bible points to Jesus, the *Son* of God.

We gain a deeper love, respect, and excitement for the Word of God when we see how the old and the new connect. This is what Jesus was doing on the road to Emmaus with his disciples. As he said, "Every *Torah* scholar discipled for the kingdom of heaven is like a master of a household who brings out of his treasure both new things and old" (Matthew 13:52).

From the very first word of the Bible, we see that Creation was made through the Messiah—that he was the agent of Creation. As John wrote, "In the beginning was the Word. The Word was with God, and the Word was God. He was with God in the beginning. All things were made through Him, and apart from Him nothing was made that has come into being" (John 1:1–3).

God saw that sin and sickness would come into the world. In his grace and mercy, before the foundation of the world, he had already determined that Jesus, the Messiah, was going to die for humanity's sins. This is what is being spoken of in the very first word of Genesis 1.

The first messianic prophecy in Scripture is found in Genesis 3:15. God promises to raise up a redeemer through the Seed of the woman who will reverse the curse and restore the blessing. This is an overarching theme of the Scripture and important for understanding Jesus' life and death. He is the Seed of the woman—the second Adam.

Jesus' hands were pierced because humans stole from the tree. His feet were pierced to fulfill the promise that the heel of the messianic Seed would crush the serpent's head. His pierced side made atonement for the sin of Eve, the one taken from man's side. The crown of thorns represents Jesus taking the curse of creation on his head to reverse it and restore the blessing.

Every Hebrew word has a numerical value, and often those values reveal deeper truths about the Scriptures. We find this in the Creation account with the number 6:

6 = number of man (humans created on the sixth day)
6 = number of the physical universe (six directions)
6 = day on which man fell (in Jewish thought)

"The number six tells not only of labor, but of 'labor and sorrow,' and it specifically marks all that is 'under the sun,' all that is 'not of God.' "[1]

Vav is the sixth letter of the Hebrew alphabet. It appears at the beginning of the sixth Hebrew word of Genesis 1:1, where it functions as the conjunction "and." *Vav* connects "heavens" and "earth." When Adam and Eve sinned, they broke the *vav*, the connection between heaven and earth, which again, according to Jewish tradition, happened on the sixth day (a Friday).

Jesus died on the sixth day to restore the connection (*vav*) so that life—abundant life—and blessing can flow back to us. Jesus came to restore the connection between heaven and earth.

The world, the flesh, and the enemy wants to make us feel that we have no value. But we have to understand that we are God's *creation*. We were made with wisdom.

DISCUSS

Now it's your turn. Take a few minutes in your group to discuss what you just watched. Use the following questions to jump-start your discussion, and make sure to read the

7

Scripture passages. Be open to receive what God is teaching you and doing in your group.

1. What part of Rabbi Jason's teaching stood out to you in this session on the mysteries of the Messiah in the story of Creation and the Fall?

2. Read John 1:1–3 and Genesis 1:1–3. What similarities do you find between these two passages? How do these connections help you see Messiah in the Genesis account? How do you feel these connections helped John's audience see Jesus?

3. Read Colossians 1:18–20. What words does the apostle Paul use to describe Jesus in these verses? How do these words and phrases connect Jesus to Creation?

4. Re-read Genesis 1:1 and 3:15. In Genesis 1:1, the Hebrew letter *vav* connects the "heavens" and the "earth." When Adam and Eve sinned, they broke the *vav,* the connection, which resulted in a curse. But even as God was issuing this curse, He was promising a way to restore the broken connection. What was that promise?

5. Read Jeremiah 10:12, Isaiah 45:7, and Matthew 10:29–31. The story of the Fall reveals that God was at work from the start to restore humanity through the promised Messiah. He is still at work today. How does knowing that God's work never stops affect you? How does knowing he is at work give you a sense of true *shalom* [peace]?

6. God created the world by speaking—through words. Likewise, your words create worlds. What does it mean to you to speak life over yourself and over the people around you? How could speaking life change your view of yourself and of others?

RESPOND

Briefly review the outline for the session one teaching and any notes you took. In the space below, write down the most significant point you took away from this session.

PRAY

Close by praying aloud together for a few minutes, asking God to work in each person's heart as you reflect on the content of this session. Write down any specific prayer requests from your group members in the space below so you can continue praying throughout the week.

BETWEEN-SESSIONS PERSONAL STUDY

While group study is important, so is personal discovery. I've always found the more I personally dig into Scripture, the more I hear from God, the more I learn from him, the more I feel in his presence, and the more of his Word I can apply to my life. Believe me, the time you invest in personal study between each week's session will be time well spent. As a teaching messianic Rabbi and lover of Scripture, I love to continue to dig and find other mysteries or discoveries hidden in God's Word. (As I often like to say, there's *more*!)

GOD HAD A PLAN FROM THE BEGINNING

Read Genesis 1:1. The first word in Hebrew is *bereisheet.* What's interesting is the first three letters of this word are *bet, resh,* and *aleph.* The second Hebrew word is *bara,* which means "God created out of nothing." The word *bara* also begins with the same first three letters: *bet, resh,* and *aleph.* This is another mystery, because these three letters are an illusion to the Trinity. *Bet* is the Son. *Resh* is the *Ruach* (the Holy Spirit). *Aleph* is the Abba (the Father).

Messiah was present at Creation with God and the Holy Spirit to create a world "out of nothing" . . . and they had a plan. On the first day of Creation, the earth was in an uninhabitable state of darkness and chaos. Biblically, chaos and darkness represent evil, exile, and death. God's goodness and abundant blessing cannot be fully manifested as long as chaos is on the earth. He must bring order out of chaos so that life can flourish. So his plan involved bringing order out of the chaos. This is true for Creation, our lives, and for the church, "for God is not a God of confusion, but *shalom* [peace]" (1 Corinthians 14:33).

1. Read Genesis 1:2–5 and 26–28. What was God's plan to start bringing order out of the chaos? What was the culmination of that plan? What was unique about the creation of humankind?

2. Read John 1:1–3. John writes that Jesus, the Messiah, was there "in the beginning." Why was it important for John to make people aware of this truth? Why is it important for you to know that Jesus—the Messiah—was with God at the very beginning of Creation?

3. Read Psalm 37:23 and 1 Corinthians 2:9. God has plans for each of us. In fact, from the *very beginning* he has had a plan—and he calls his plans good. He has plans for you as well—and he calls those plans good. How have you seen God's good plans at work in your life?

BRINGING ORDER OUT OF CHAOS

God has the power to bring order out of chaos and light out of darkness. God, Messiah, and the Holy Spirit created order in the world so humanity could experience abundant blessing and life. However, when Adam and Eve sinned, disorder and chaos were no longer fully restrained. Rather, chaos and disorder became an ever-present reality that increased in strength over time as humanity, due to its fallen state, continued to reject the Lord and his ways.

The rabbis say that God created the world for the sake of the Messiah, because he saw that sin and sickness would come into the world. God, in his grace and mercy, wasn't going to create the world if there wasn't already a cure and an antidote in place before the curse of sin and death came into the world. In Jewish thought, God went to the Messiah and said, "I'll only create the world if you are willing to suffer and die for the sake of redeeming my people."

God's blueprint, his plan, is to bring order out of the chaos caused by sin and bring redemption. And he had this idea from the *very first word* of Genesis.

4. One of the best examples of redemption is God saving Israel from Egyptian bondage. In Exodus, God redeems Israel from suffering and saves them from slavery to bring them to the Promised Land. How does God's redemption of Israel compare to the antidote provided by Jesus?

5. Read Jesus' words in Mark 10:45. To *redeem* (or *redemption*) means to purchase back something. The word always means a "ransom" or a "price paid." What was the price Jesus paid for us? How does paying this ransom clear the chaos and bring order?

6. The apostle Paul wrote in Ephesians 1:7, "In Him [Yeshua] we have redemption through His blood—the removal of trespasses—in keeping with the richness of His grace." How does Jesus' redemption bring us out of darkness? What are the results of his redemption?

WHAT HIS PLAN MEANS FOR YOU

Read Colossians 1:16 and 1 Corinthians 8:6. In this session, you learned how Messiah was part of Creation and how God has an individual plan for each of us that includes freeing us from chaos and exile through Jesus' redemptive act on the cross. God created the world, and when he did, he already had a plan in place to free us from the evil and sin that lead us to disorder and chaos. His plan was Jesus, who was with him from the beginning.

7. How would you describe chaos? In what ways do chaos and disorder keep you from God's full blessing in your life?

8. How does the Creation story help you to clearly see the power, knowledge, and wisdom of the Creator God and his redemptive plan with Jesus?

9. Read John 14:27. Jesus brings order out of chaos. Managing and bringing order out of chaos may seem daunting, whatever your circumstances may be. How can Jesus help you to walk and live in his *shalom*—his peace?

10. Read Psalm 119:105. One of the critical components of overcoming chaos in your life and restoring order is God's Word. We need the wisdom, power, and light of God's Word to help us overcome the potentially damaging spiritual, emotional, and relational harm caused by the chaos in our lives. What could you set aside so that you have time to study God's Word?

11. Read Proverbs 2:6, 3:13, and 5:1. What do you need to start removing some of the chaos and disorder from your life?

For Next Week: In the next session, you will explore the mysteries of the Messiah as told in the stories of the Jewish patriarchs—Abraham, Isaac, and Jacob. These men were critical to the history of the Jewish people, so it is important for you to know them and understand their connection to the Messiah. Before your group gathers, read chapters 2–3 in *Mysteries of the Messiah.* Also take a few minutes to acquaint or reacquaint yourself with these three important men and their families by reviewing Genesis 11–12, 17, 21–22, and 25.

Note

1. E. W. Bullinger, *Number in Scripture: Its Supernatural Design and Spiritual Significance* (London, Eyre & Spottiswoode [Bible Warehouse] Ltd., 1921), 102.

FINDING JESUS IN THE STORY OF THE PATRIARCHS

The promised Seed of the woman began to find its fulfillment in Abraham and his offspring. The call and mission of the patriarchs reflect God's original intention for humankind: to experience God's blessing and be a conduit of that blessing to the world. God handpicked Abraham, Isaac, and Jacob to play a foundational role in birthing the line of the chosen Seed, who would reverse the curse and bring about the new Eden.

WELCOME

In the previous session, we examined the mysteries of the Messiah as revealed in the story of Creation. We discussed how God promised the Messiah—the One who would reverse the curse of the Fall—would come through the "Seed" of the woman (see Genesis 3:15). This promised Seed would ultimately come through the *patriarchs*—through the line of Abraham, Isaac, and Jacob.

The Jewish people trace their ancestry back to one man: **Abraham,** the "founding father" of Israel (see Isaiah 51:2; Hebrews 7:4). In the history of the Jewish people, the father of a family was held in high esteem. He retained authority over his children and grandchildren until his death. Families were united under a common head, with the eldest son honored with great dignity. Abraham left Mesopotamia and its idols behind and journeyed, at God's direction, to the land of Canaan. It is estimated that he lived from 2165 BC to 1992 BC.

The title of *patriarch* was passed from Abraham to his son **Isaac**, whose name means "laugh." This commemorated Abraham's joyous response to the news that Sarah was pregnant (see Genesis 17:17–19). His birth meant that the everlasting covenant God made with Abraham would go on to the next generations of Isaac's descendants. Later, God told Abraham to take this beloved son to the land of Moriah and offer him as a burnt sacrifice (see Genesis 22). It is estimated that Isaac lived from 2067 BC to 1887 BC.

Isaac was sixty when his twin sons, Esau and Jacob, were born. **Jacob,** the second son, came out of the womb grasping his brother's heel, appearing to be trying to hold his brother back and be the first born. Some interpret his name to mean "heel grabber." Jacob deceived his father, grabbed the birthright of the firstborn, and spent much of his life in fear of his brother, Esau. He was the father of Joseph and had the distinction of wrestling with God, breaking his hip, and being transformed to be named Israel (meaning "God contends," "one who struggles with God," and "Prince of God"). It is estimated he lived from 1916 BC to 1807 BC.[1]

These three men—Abraham, Isaac, and Jacob—became the roots of the ancestral tree of the nation of Israel. "The patriarchs were wealthy nomads, though occasionally they farmed (Genesis 26:12). With the exception of a burial site at Hebron (Genesis 23) and the region of Shechem (Genesis 33:18–34:31; 48:22), they did not own land."[2]

The patriarchs were tasked with carrying on the religious traditions of their fathers. They were the vehicles through which the revelation of God was made available to their families and communities. Each one passed the baton of faith in God to the succeeding generation. Perhaps each one told the faith stories about Creation, the Fall, Noah, Enoch, and others to their children and grandchildren. They held firm to God's guiding promise and worshiped the One who would lead, guard, prosper, and protect them. As we will see in this session, they are key figures in our quest to uncover the mysteries of the Messiah.

SHARE

If your group members are just getting to know one another, take a few minutes to introduce yourselves. Before you watch the video teaching, pair up with another member (perhaps someone you don't know that well) and briefly discuss the following questions:

- Many families have varied backgrounds, and often certain family members stand out over others. Who in your family has been like a patriarch? What legacy or ideals did that person pass along to you?

- God made a promise with Abraham. This promise, known as the Abrahamic Covenant, is the foundation for Israel's covenant with God. What does a promise or vow mean to you?

WATCH

Watch the video for session two. (Play the DVD or see the instructions on the inside front cover on how to access the sessions through streaming.) As you watch, use the following outline to record any thoughts or concepts that stand out to you.

Abraham demonstrated his faith in God by going through ten tests. The first test was the calling of Abraham in Genesis 12:1. The word "go" in Hebrew is *lech lecha*, which means "go to yourself." Abraham had to leave behind his past in order to step forward into his future.

Abraham's final test, known as the binding of Isaac, is found in Genesis 22:2. The verse begins with the same words: *lech lecha*. Once again, God is essentially saying to Abraham, "You trusted me with your past. Will you trust me with your future—with Isaac, the promised Seed?"

Abraham places the wood for the burnt offering on Isaac, and he carries it himself. This is like Jesus carrying the crossbeam for his own crucifixion. Even the rabbis make this connection when they say in the Midrash, "Like a man who carries his own cross."

The number 134 has great significance in the story of the binding of Isaac:

134 = his cross
134 = I sacrificed to the Lord
134 = pardon for sin

Jesus would later carry *his cross* because he was going to offer himself as a *sacrifice to the Lord* so that you and I could receive *pardon for sin.*

The blood of Isaac is connected to the blood of the Passover lamb, which ultimately points to the blood of Jesus, the true Lamb of God. Jesus is the Lamb of God who was slain before the foundations of the world so that we could be forgiven, freed, and redeemed.

God told Abraham, "Take your son, your only son whom you love . . . and offer him . . . as a burnt offering" (Genesis 22:2). The numeric value of "as a burnt offering" (*olah*) is 135, the same as *matzah*, the unleavened bread the Lord commanded the children of Israel to eat at the Passover. Isaac is portrayed as a Passover lamb and as a type of Messiah.

Jacob's name means "supplanter" or "heel." In English, a heel is a person who steps on others to get ahead in life. At first, Jacob was willing to use any means necessary to obtain the coveted blessing. Just like Abraham, he had to go on a journey of transformation.

Ultimately, Jacob realizes that the One he must wrestle with is the Lord himself. When he wrestles with God, he is transformed and has his named changed to "Israel"—which means "one who overcomes" or "Prince of God." He also ends up walking with a limp.

Jacob had a life-changing encounter on his way to Haran. He dreamed of "a ladder standing earthward and its top reached the heaven [Genesis 28:12]."[3] The ladder [sulam] is a vehicle of revelation, the means by which heaven and earth communicate.

130 = ladder
130 = Sinai
130 = God's voice

Jesus is the ladder [sulam] that connects heaven and earth. The same voice that spoke to the children of Israel at Sinai speaks to us through Jesus the Messiah.

Jacob had a promise, but he had to go through a process. God had to break Jacob before he could bless him. The same is true for every one of us. God has to break us before he can make us. There has to be brokenness before there can be blessing in our lives.

When Moses came down from Mount Sinai and saw the people committing the sin of the golden calf, he took the Ten Commandments and smashed them to pieces. Ultimately God forgave the children of Israel and gave Moses a second set. This teaches us that brokenness comes out of wholeness. Nothing is as whole as a broken heart.

The first set of tablets point to the first coming of the Messiah. Jesus was broken for us on the cross because of our sin. The second set point to the second coming of Christ. Jesus is going to do away with sin, pain, and sickness. But even as we wait, we can still experience wholeness out of brokenness through our Yeshua Jesus, our Messiah.

DISCUSS

Now it's your turn. Take a few minutes in your group to discuss what you just watched. Use the following questions to jump-start your discussion, and make sure to read the Scripture passages. Be open to receive what God is teaching you and doing in your group.

1. In this session, we looked at the founders of the Jewish people—Abraham, Isaac, and Jacob. What stood out to you in this teaching? What can you apply to your life today?

2. Read Genesis 12:1 and Genesis 22:1–2. As discussed in this session, the word translated "go" is the Hebrew word *lech lecha,* meaning "go to yourself." God asked Abraham to embark (go) toward the ultimate purpose he had for him. When was a time in your life when God told you to *lech lecha* (go) for his purpose?

3. Read Ephesians 1:7–9. When God tested Abraham in Genesis 12, he was saying, "Abraham, will you trust Me with your past?" By later offering Isaac (see Genesis 22), God was asking Abraham, "Will you give Me your future?" Why

is it important to trust your past to God? What tends to keep you from trusting your future to him?

4. Isaac needed to have great faith and courage to completely trust his father and allow himself to be offered as a sacrifice. What insights and connections did you discover during the teaching from Isaac as a type (a "prophetic symbol") of the Messiah?

5. Jacob wrestled with his brother (see Genesis 25; 27), with his father (see Genesis 27) , and with his father-in-law (Genesis 29–31). But ultimately, he needed to wrestle with the Lord to receive the promised blessing (see Genesis 32). When was a time you wrestled with God over a decision or a turning point in your life journey?

6. Read Genesis 28:10–17, John 1:43–51, and Philippians 3:12–14. Jesus is the *ladder*—the one who connects heaven and earth. How does this vision of the ladder parallel spiritual progress? In what ways do you climb the ladder daily and connect with Jesus?

RESPOND

Briefly review the outline for the session two teaching and any notes you took. In the space below, write down the most significant point you took away from this session.

PRAY

Close by praying aloud together for a few minutes, asking God to work in each person's heart as you reflect on the content of this session. Write down any specific prayer requests from your group members in the space below so you can continue praying throughout the week.

BETWEEN-SESSIONS PERSONAL STUDY

A s I often like to say, there's *more*! In our first session, we studied the mystery of Jesus in Creation. The promised Seed of the woman (see Genesis 3:15) began to find its fulfillment in Abraham and his offspring. The call and mission of the patriarchs reflect God's original intention for humankind: to experience God's blessing and to be a conduit of blessing to the world. God handpicked Abraham, Isaac, and Jacob to play a foundational role in birthing the line of the chosen Seed promised in Creation. But these fathers of the faith faced many challenges as well.

ABRAHAM'S FAITH AND TRANSFORMATION

Read Genesis 11:31 and 12:1–5. God tells Abraham *lech lecha*— "Get going out from your land, and from your relatives, and from your father's house, to the land that I will show you" (Genesis 12:1). It's interesting to note that God could have said just "*lech*" to Abraham—to just "go" out of the land. But he didn't. As we studied in this session, *lech lecha* means "go to yourself." Another meaning is that God was telling

Abraham to "go inside yourself." Many of us are not called to leave our native land and go to a strange place, but we are called to go, with Yeshua, on an inward journey of testing that opens the door to increased faith and transformation.

1. As you read Genesis 12:1–5, notice that Abraham had to take a step of faith. So often we want a roadmap, but God wants us to let him direct the first step . . . and then the next step. Sometimes the "next step" doesn't come quickly, and God asks us to wait. Can you describe a time when God asked you to wait? How did it feel? What was your response?

2. Abraham obeyed when God told him to go and ultimately faced ten tests. Jesus also obeyed God, setting aside his heavenly position to come to the earth as a man (see Luke 19:10; John 3:16–17; 1 John 4:9). Jesus also faced many tests during his short time on earth. Both Abraham and Jesus were called by God, responded to God's call, and accomplished (finished) what they were called to do. Can you see the connection between Abraham finishing his calling and Jesus? How does it affect your faith to know Jesus finished what he came to do?

3. Read John 16:33 and Luke 21:16–19. You, like Abraham and Jesus, will encounter opposition as you seek to go and do what God has called you to do. There are four purposes for such testing: (1) to humble you, (2) to bring you closer to Jesus, (3) to test your faith, and (4) to equip you to help other people (after all, how can you relate to the needs of others if you don't experience testing?). How do you see these purposes played out in the story of God asking Abraham to sacrifice Isaac? How might the experience have humbled him and brought him closer to God? How has testing humbled you and yet helped you minister to others?

JACOB'S FAITH AND TRANSFORMATION

In Genesis 28:10, we read, "Then Jacob left Beer-sheba and went toward Haran." The name Beer-sheba means "Well of the Seven." In Hebrew, the number seven represents process, progress, completion, and time (such as the seven days of the week). Haran means "anger" and symbolizes the barriers that prevent people from reaching higher levels of spiritual growth. Jacob's journey from Beer-sheba to Haran thus points to the process Jacob went through to progress to a new spiritual level. For Jacob, this culminated in him wrestling with God during the night and emerging with victory, but also with an injury (see Genesis 32:24–32).

4. One of the mysteries of the Messiah is that Jesus would come through the line of the patriarchs—which included men with faults such as Jacob. This man grabbed at his brother's heel at his birth. He tricked his father to receive the birthright. He used earthly means to try and secure the promise. What does it say that God chose to use men like Jacob in spite of these failings? What does that say about the kinds of people whom he uses today?

5. Why is it often so tempting to rely on earthly means to obtain God's promises? What are some of the consequences that occur when you take that approach?

6. "God meets us at whatever level He finds us in order to lift us to where He wants us to be. To Abraham the pilgrim, God came as a traveler (Genesis 18); and to Joshua the general, He came as a soldier (Joshua 5:13–15). Jacob had spent most of his adult life wrestling with people—Esau, Isaac, Laban, and even his wives—so God came to him as a wrestler."[4] In what way has God found you? How has his perfect approach to who he made you to be helped you in your spiritual transformation?

7. Read 2 Corinthians 12:6–10. The process of spiritual transformation can make you bitter or better. And it's often a scary process, because what God does will be out of your control. Any attempts to shorten the process will only lead to delays that hinder the results—the blessing. How you respond to God's process is essential to your growth. What was Paul's response to the process of the "thorn"? Do you sense that he was wrestling with God or freely accepting the process and the potential of blessing for his perseverance? Explain.

8. The easy way will not lead to the blessing. Sometimes, you need to wrestle a bit. In the New Testament, we read how Satan offered Jesus, the Messiah, the easy path without the process (see Matthew 4:1–11). But Yeshua knew he couldn't go from the cross to the empty tomb through such means. What ammunition did Jesus use against Satan's short-cut plan?

9. What is your best protection against Satan's attacks when it comes to God's process of spiritual transformation in your life?

WHAT FAITH AND TRANSFORMATION MEANS FOR YOU

Both Abraham and Jacob went through processes that lead to increased faith and transformation in their lives. Abraham experienced ten tests, with the ultimate one being to "go" and sacrifice his promised son, Isaac. Jacob, the deceiver and schemer, wrestled with God. The process left him with a broken hip, but also a new name. He went from deceiver to Israel—the one who wrestled with God and won! Both men experienced different processes but came away blessed and transformed. Likewise, God will call you to go through processes. His heart is to increase your faith and transform you into the image of Jesus. If you persevere in this process, you will grow. You will ascend to the blessings that God has for you.

10. Read Philippians 3:12–14 and Genesis 28:10–15. Recall that in Jacob's dream of the ladder, the rungs represent spiritual progress. If you become a victim to your circumstances or opinions of others, you will become bitter and lower yourself on the ladder of spiritual progress. However, if you rely on God's grace, Jesus' example, and the power of the Holy Spirit, you can climb the ladder daily. Paul was taking hold of the ladder's rungs and pressing into a heavenly goal. How do you think Paul could press on in the midst of the "pressing"?

11. How has studying God's Word helped you through the process of climbing the ladder?

12. Read 1 Peter 1:6–7. Remember that Peter denied Jesus three times during the night of Jesus' trial. However, after the resurrection, Yeshua took special care to help and forgive Peter and assure him that he was forgiven (see John 21:15–23). How do you think Peter might have wrestled with God during the time between Jesus' trial and resurrection?

13. Peter's use of "various trials" literally means "varied, multi-colored, or diversified" trials. What process do you think God had for Peter's transformation in his life? What do you think Peter learned from the process? What do you learn from God's process in your life?

14. Abraham left his homeland because God told him to *go*. His faith was built on several important truths. The first is that God is "the faithful God" (Deuteronomy 7:9). Additionally, Abraham knew God was good (see Psalm 136:1) and loving (see 1 John 4:8). He knew that he could trust God completely because God loved him, knew what was best for him, and would act with his best interests in mind. How have you seen this at work in your life? What blessings have you received when you have chosen to trust God and *go* where he leads?

15. Read Mark 16:15. Jesus told his disciples to "go." It is as if he's saying, "I've taught you, you've learned from Me, I am going to use you. Now GET GOING!" What have you learned from the story of the patriarchs—Abraham, Isaac, and Jacob—and Messiah that will help you to trust God, withstand the process, and achieve what he has called you to do?

For Next Week: In the next session, you will explore the mysteries of the Messiah as revealed in the stories of Joseph and Judah. Before your group gathers, read chapter 4 in *Mysteries of the Messiah.* Also take a few minutes to acquaint or reacquaint yourself with these two important men by reviewing the events told in Genesis 37–50.

Notes

1. Estimated life dates are from James E. Smith, *Old Testament Survey Series: The Pentateuch* (Joplin, MO: College Press, 1992, 1993), Logos Bible Software Edition.
2. Edward Bridge, "Patriarchs," in *The Lexham Bible Dictionary*, eds. John D. Barry, et al. (Bellingham, WA: Lexham Press, 2016).
3. Baal Haturim Chumash, vol. 1, *Bereishis* (Brooklyn, NY: Mesorah Publications, 1999), 253.
4. Warren W. Wiersbe, *Be Authentic*, "Be" Commentary Series (Colorado Springs, CO: Chariot Victor Pub., 1997), 58.

FINDING JESUS IN THE STORIES OF JOSEPH AND JUDAH

In Jewish thought, the stories of Joseph and Judah lead to the belief that there are two Messiahs. The first is Messiah, son of Joseph. He is pictured as the suffering Messiah, who must endure trials on his journey to fulfill God's plans. The second is Messiah, son of Judah. He is the messianic king who is going to come into the world to rule and to reign. In truth, the stories of Joseph and Judah reveal the first and second comings of Christ. He came into the world as a suffering servant, but will one day return as a conquering king.

WELCOME

Joseph and Judah were part of a large family. Rivalry, jealousy, and ultimately reconciliation characterized the relationship between these brothers—and the relationships within the entire family as well. However, in between the pages of their story, we find mysteries of the Messiah are revealed. But before we explore those connections, let's set the scene.

We spent some time in the last session learning about Jacob. He was the younger son of Isaac and Rebekah, the twin brother of Esau, and the man who wrestled with God and had his name changed to Israel (see Genesis 25–35). Jacob's journey, unlike Abraham, was not a result of God calling him to "go." Rather, Jacob, the schemer, needed to escape his brother, who wanted to kill him. At his mother's urging, Jacob left home to go live with his uncle Laban.

It turns out that Uncle Laban was even more of a schemer than Jacob. Laban connived to have Jacob stay and work for him for more than a decade. It took Jacob seven years to earn the hand of Rachel, Laban's daughter. But as a result of more scheming by Laban, Jacob found himself married to two sisters, Leah and Rachel. After *twenty* years, God appeared to Jacob and told him to return to the land of his birthplace (see Genesis 31:3).

Jacob's family eventually grew to twelve sons and one daughter:

- **Children by Leah:** Reuben, Simeon, Levi, Judah, Issachar, Zebulun, and Dinah
- **Children by Bilhah** (Rachel's handmaid): Dan and Naphtali

- **Children by Zilpah** (Leah's handmaid): Gad and Asher
- **Children by Rachel:** Joseph and Benjamin

Jacob did not treat each of these children equally. He held Joseph dearer than his other children, as he was a child of Rachel, who had experienced trouble in becoming pregnant. At the time the events in Genesis 37 unfold, Joseph was the youngest. Jacob's indulgences toward this favored son led to jealousy from the other sons. In their bitterness and rage, they sold Joseph to traders, who eventually took him to Egypt and sold him as a slave.

Judah was not the firstborn of Jacob—that distinction fell to Reuben. However, after Rachel's death, "Reuben went and slept with his father's concubine Bilhah, and [Jacob] heard about it" (Genesis 35:22). This resulted in Jacob, on his deathbed, conferring the leadership of Israel not on Reuben, as was the custom, but on Judah.

From this somewhat dysfunctional family came two brothers, each of whom—as we will discover in this session—has major connections to the Messiah.

SHARE

Before you watch the video teaching, pair up with another member and briefly discuss the following questions:

- Struggles between family members are just a part of family life. What is a funny story that you can tell about an argument you had with a sibling when you were young? What happened in that situation?

- Of course, there is more to family life than just struggles! What do you think your family "got right" when it came to the way you were raised? Share a bit about your background, how you grew up, and your parents' values.

WATCH

Watch the video for session three. (Play the DVD or see the instructions on the inside front cover on how to access the sessions through streaming.) As you watch, use the following outline to record any thoughts or concepts that stand out to you.

Joseph and Judah play a significant role in understanding the person and work of the Messiah. In Jewish thought there are actually two Messiahs: (1) Messiah, son of Joseph (the suffering servant), and (2) Messiah, son of Judah (the ruling king). These two aspects of the Messiah are revealed in the lives of these two key individuals in the book of Genesis.

One practical takeaway from the story of Joseph is that whenever you have a God-given dream, there are always going to be haters. There are going to be people who mock your dreams. But you can't kill a God dream. A God dream will always come to pass.

There are many amazing parallels between Joseph and Jesus:

Joseph	Jesus
rejected by his brothers	rejected by his family
sold for silver	betrayed for silver
betrayed by "Judah"	betrayed by "Judas"
cast lots for tunic	cast lots for clothing
raised from a pit (actual pit)	raised from the "pit" (the grave)
overcame temptation	overcame temptation
falsely accused	falsely accused
leadership at age thirty	leadership at age thirty

Furthermore, the first time Joseph's brothers came to Egypt, they didn't recognize him. In the same way, the Jewish people of Jesus' day didn't recognize him as the Messiah at his first coming. But at the *second coming*, all Israel will be saved, as Paul writes in Romans 11. God will one day open the eyes of Israel—and this will lead to the opening of the eyes of all the nations.

Joseph had two sons: Manasseh and Ephraim. The name Manasseh means, "I have forgotten the pain of my past." The name Ephraim means, "double fruitfulness." If we can't forgive and forget, we will never be fruitful. When we can't forgive, we bitter the fruit at the root, and it contaminates every aspect of our lives. One of the greatest obstacles to finding freedom in Jesus is unforgiveness.

When Jacob blessed his sons, he gave a seminal prophecy about the Messiah: "The scepter will not pass from Judah, nor the ruler's staff from between his feet, until he to whom it belongs will come. To him will be the obedience of the peoples" (Genesis 49:10). This prophecy provides the time-frame of the coming of the Messiah.

The *staff* represents tribal identity. The *scepter* represents judicial authority. The Messiah would come between the time Israel lost judicial authority and tribal identity. Judicial authority lost in 3 BC (at the Roman occupation). Tribal identity was lost in AD 70 (when the Romans destroyed the Temple). This is exactly the time that Jesus was born, lived, and ministered.

In fact, there are not *two* Messiahs, but two *comings* of the Messiah. The first time he came as Messiah, Son of Joseph, the suffering servant and the Lamb of God. He will return the second time as the Son of David, the warrior Messiah and conquering King, who—like his ancestor David—will usher in a time of *shalom* (peace) and blessing as the Lion of Judah.

The messianic King was to come from the tribe of Judah, and that King had to be born in Bethlehem. Why is that so significant? The number 490 reveals the answer:

490 = *Beit Lechem* (Bethlehem / house of bread)
490 = *moladati* (nativity)
490 = *tamim* (complete, whole, perfect)

"This great man [Joseph], though not as yet known to them to be their brother, determined to forgive their mistreatment and, instead demonstrate great grace. . . . This reunion [with his brothers] was really a banquet of grace—on full display—thanks to Joseph, a man of integrity and forgiveness."[1]

Just as we can't live physically without bread, we can't live spiritually and relationally without the bread of forgiveness. When we withhold forgiveness from someone, it is like telling a starving person to go and die. Our hearts cannot be perfect or completely whole before the Lord unless we are willing to follow Jesus' example and forgive others.

Forgiveness leads to freedom, blessing, and fruitfulness. So, who do you need to forgive in your life? Maybe it's someone who wronged you. Maybe it's even yourself. It doesn't make a difference. Simply *forgive* . . . and you will be blessed.

DISCUSS

Now it's your turn. Take a few minutes in your group to discuss what you just watched. Use the following questions to jump-start your discussion and make sure to read the Scripture passages. Be open to receive what God is teaching you and doing in your group.

1. The stories of Joseph and Judah have tremendous application to our lives today as followers of Christ. What in particular in this lesson stood out to you? Why?

2. Read Genesis 37:1–11. God has a dream for your life, and that dream is unique to you—no one else on earth can fulfill it. Like Joseph, your God-dream contains your purpose and reason for being. Has God shared his dream for you with you? Have you shared your dreams with God and submitted them to him? Why or why not?

3. Read John 11:53 and 15:25. There are many parallels between Jesus and Joseph. What is the prophetic significance of these parallels? How do they picture the first and second coming of Christ? What do you find as the most significant parallel?

4. *Manasseh* in Hebrew means, "I have forgotten the pain of my past." *Ephraim* means, "double fruitfulness." What do these names teach you?

5. Read Genesis 49:8–12. Jacob's blessing reveals secrets about both the first and the second coming of Messiah. What are those secrets? How do they connect to Jesus as the Messiah? How do they help you to understand the "end of days"?

6. Read Genesis 50:15–21 and Matthew 18:21–22. Forgiveness is not an *option* but a *requirement*—not to stress us but to bless us. How do you think Joseph could forgive his brothers? What is the significance of Jesus telling Peter that he needed to forgive seven times seventy times? Who is it today that *you* need to forgive?

RESPOND

Briefly review the outline for the session three teaching and any notes you took. In the space below, write down the most significant point you took away from this session.

PRAY

Close by praying aloud together for a few minutes, asking God to work in each person's heart as you reflect on the content of this session. Write down any specific prayer requests from your group members in the space below so you can continue praying throughout the week.

BETWEEN-SESSIONS PERSONAL STUDY

The life of Joseph paints a powerful picture that fore-shadows the Messiah's coming rejection and suffering. In fact, in Jewish tradition, the suffering Messiah is referred to as "Messiah, Son of Joseph" (*Mashiach Ben Yosef*). An examination of Joseph's life reveals that what happened to the *first* Joseph also happened to the *second* Joseph (Jesus). During this week's small-group time, you examined several parallels between Joseph and Jesus. In this personal study, you will dive a bit deeper (there's always more!) into two of those parallels.

JOSEPH AND JESUS WERE REJECTED

Joseph's brothers plotted against him out of envy and jealousy. Likewise, the religious leaders of Jesus' day—who *should* have recognized him as the Messiah—plotted to kill him. Both Joseph and Jesus were rejected and betrayed by their own people.

God created us for acceptance. When we are rejected, we feel abandoned, unaccepted, and deep hurt. Feelings of rejection can stop us from moving forward. Our enemy, Satan, loves to use this against us. He wants to twist our thoughts away from God and toward bitterness, isolation, and pain. Rejection can be a test of our faith.

Both Joseph and Jesus passed the test. They moved on from rejection because God was their first thought. As one theologian noted, "In studying the character of Joseph we have seen that its single most distinguishing feature was his ability to relate everything to God. God was in his thoughts constantly. There is hardly a sentence from his lips that does not have the name of God in it."[2] I think we can say the same feature applies to Jesus (see John 10:30).

1. Read Genesis 37:18–30, Matthew 26:14–16, and 27:28–35. It is Reuben who suggests the brothers throw Joseph into a pit. Before doing so, they strip Joseph of the special tunic that his father had given him. Judah then suggests they sell Joseph for twenty pieces of silver to some travelling Ishmaelite slave traders. What parallels do you see between these incidents in Joseph's life as told in Genesis and the life of Jesus as told in Matthew?

2. Read Genesis 39:6–20 and 40:20–23. Joseph's circumstances go from bad to worse in Egypt, yet he continues to trust in the Lord. He had previously been rejected by his

brothers, but kept his focus on God. Potiphar's wife puts him in a compromising position, but he refuses to sin and flees from the room. He is sent to prison and suffers negative consequences for doing what was right, yet he keeps his mind and heart on God. Later, he is forgotten by the chief cupbearer and languishes another two years in prison. But God continues to work in the background—and Joseph continues to trust in him. Ultimately, Joseph goes from the prison to the palace. As you look at his story, how have you been rejected by family, others, or friends? How did you overcome those feelings? What have been some circumstances in your life that seemed impossible until you saw God working in the background to bring victory?

3. Read Genesis 45:5–9. These verses reveal Joseph's incredible focus on God. Instead of harboring anger or resentment toward his brothers, he allays their fears and four times points them to God. Underline or write out those four references to God. How did Joseph's focus on the Lord stabilize his perspective on life? How did this focus help him to forgive his brothers?

4. Read John 14:1–7 and 1 John 4:18. Jesus was surrounded by rejection, false accusations, and persecution. He knew that his followers would experience the same. What does Jesus promise to those who trust in him? What does Jesus say about allowing your heart to "be troubled"? What does it mean to you that God's "perfect love drives out fear"?

JOSEPH AND JESUS SAVED NATIONS

When Joseph interprets Pharaoh's dreams (see Genesis 41), it results not only in the salvation of Egypt but also of the nation of Israel. Furthermore, we find that Joseph not only saves his people *physically* (by allowing them to overcome the lean years), but he also saves them *spiritually* (through his act of forgiveness toward his brothers). When Joseph finally reveals himself to them, he doesn't hold a grudge or try to get even against them (see Genesis 45).

Jesus later summed up his own nation-saving desire when he told Nicodemus, "For God so loved *the world* that He gave His one and only Son, that whoever believes in Him *shall not perish* but have eternal life. God did not send His Son into the world to condemn the world, but *in order that the world might be saved through Him*" (John 3:16–17, emphasis added).

5. Read Genesis 37:1–11 and 39:1–23. Like many of the Bible stories, we don't get a glimpse of Joseph's feelings. But we can read between the lines of the text and realize that Joseph's years of trials were well endured by this man of dreams. He grew spiritually through each challenge. How do you think it was possible for Joseph to maintain his love for God and not lose hope?

6. Potiphar's wife in Joseph's story represents an attack against our God-given dreams. How did Joseph's response develop his character for his true calling to save nations? How are your God-given dreams attacked? How have you persevered to keep doing what God has called you to do?

7. Read Genesis 41:15–16. Just as Joseph never became despondent when his circumstances took a turn for the worse, so he did not become arrogant and prideful when things took a turn for the good. What enabled Joseph to keep from falling into arrogance?

8. Read Luke 4:18 and Mark 3:20–30. Pharaoh was not only impressed with *what* Joseph did (interpret dreams), but he also had an accurate sense of *how* Joseph did it (by the Spirit of God). One of Jesus' first public acts was the reading of the Scripture in Nazareth. Like Joseph, he did what he did by the Spirit of God. How does the Spirit of God lead you today? Why is it impossible for you to try and fulfill your God-given dream *without* God's help?

WHAT REJECTION AND SAVING THE NATIONS MEANS FOR YOU

In this study, we've learned that Joseph was rejected. He was envied, thrown in a pit, and sold to slave traders by his brothers. Likewise, a critical part of the Messiah's job description required him to be rejected by his people, Israel. He would suffer, die, and be resurrected in atonement for the transgressions of Israel and the nations.

Joseph's experiences ultimately led to him to be in a position where he was able to save two nations—both Egypt and the nation of Israel. He used what he learned from God, the pit, prison, and the palace to offer forgiveness to his brothers and save the line of Messiah. Likewise, another part of the Messiah's job description was Savior. He came to rescue us and save us. His desire is for every person, worldwide, to come to him and be saved.

9. Read John 1:11 and John 5:43. Jesus was rejected by the people of his day. His hometown rejected him. The religious leaders rejected him. Even Peter at one point rejected knowing him (though he was later restored). Like Joseph, the Messiah knew what it felt to be rejected by those who were close to him. People are still rejecting him today. Our culture finds it easy to accept sports stars, movie stars, and rock stars. So why do you think so many people have difficulty accepting Jesus? What led *you* to accept Jesus?

10. Read Hebrews 4:15 and 5:8–9. Both Jesus and Joseph learned obedience through their suffering. Jesus understands us perfectly because he's been through it all—he feels what we feel. How does knowing that Jesus understands your pain, suffering, and challenges help you to confidently approach him? How does it help you, like Joseph, live under stress?

11. Read Matthew 28:16–20 and Acts 1:8. Jesus came to make it possible for *anyone* to be forgiven of their sins and be adopted into God's family. Through his life, crucifixion, resurrection, and enthronement in heaven, the way was made for the Holy Spirit to be poured out, empowering his followers to become missionaries who would share the good news everywhere. What are some of the barriers that keep you from sharing Jesus' life-saving message? How can you, like Joseph, do what God has called you to do—including telling others about him?

For Next Week: In the next session, you will explore the mysteries of the Messiah as revealed in the story of Moses and his calling by God. Before your group gathers, read chapters 5–7 in *Mysteries of the Messiah*. Also take a few minutes to acquaint or reacquaint yourself with the events of Moses' leading the people out of Egypt as told in Exodus 1–7.

Notes
1. Charles R. Swindoll, *Joseph: A Man of Integrity and Forgiveness* (Nashville: Thomas Nelson, 1998), 131.
2. James Montgomery Boice, *Genesis: An Expositional Commentary* (Grand Rapids, MI: Baker Books, 1998), 1057.

FINDING JESUS IN THE STORY OF MOSES

Moses is perhaps the most powerful portrait of the person and work of the Messiah. Even his birth was intended to be a sneak preview of the birth of the Messiah! He is the greatest prophet of the Hebrew Bible, a central figure in Judaism, and was used by God not only to free the Israelites from slavery to Egypt—the greatest superpower of its day—but also to give the Ten Commandments and the Torah to the Hebrew people. No leader or prophet is as loved and revered by the Jewish people as Moses.

WELCOME

In this session, we are going to study the mysteries of the Messiah as revealed in the story of Moses—a man whom many would call, among other admirable things, the greatest leader in Jewish history. Moses was born in the land of Goshen in Egypt (c. 1391 BC), where the Israelites had settled during the time of Joseph. The situation in Egypt had deteriorated, and the Israelites were now being forced to work as slaves. So God called Moses from a burning bush to lead the people out of Egyptian bondage and into the land that he promised to give to Abraham.

At first glance, Moses was an odd choice for the job. He had gone into hiding in the wilderness after murdering an Egyptian for beating a fellow Hebrew. By his own admonition, he was not "a man of words" because he had "a slow mouth and a heavy tongue" (Exodus 4:10). He argued against God's call and asked him to choose someone else. But God persisted that he had found the person. He saw leadership traits in Moses that Moses couldn't see himself.

As one author noted, "God . . . had a mission for Moses, and he communicated it to him in no uncertain terms: 'So now, go. I am sending you to Pharaoh to bring my people the Israelites out of Egypt' (Exodus 3:10). It was this calling that would drastically alter the trajectory of Moses' life. Like the World War II posters of Uncle Sam that called young men to enlist in the army, God was pointing his finger at Moses and saying, 'I want you!' "[1]

What traits made Moses such a great leader? In a study sponsored by the American Management Association, leadership authors and consultants James Kouzes and Barry

Posner asked this same question in a survey of nearly 1,500 managers from across the United States. "More than 225 values and traits were identified, which were then grouped into 15 categories. The number one thing respondents said they wanted most from their leaders was integrity."[2] Leadership expert John Maxwell agrees. He identifies attributes such as influence, process, empowerment, trust, and connection, to name a few, as qualities of successful leaders.[3]

Moses possessed many of these qualities that experts believe make a successful leader. He delivered his people from slavery and led a recalcitrant bunch (some estimate more than two million people) through the wilderness. He learned to delegate, he performed miracles at God's command, and his vigor, wisdom, and passion were with him throughout his life. He did all of this without falling into pride. As the Scriptures relate, "Now the man Moses was very humble, more so than anyone on the face of the earth" (Numbers 12:3).

Yet Moses had one other critical quality that made him the right person for the job: he enjoyed a singularly focused relationship with God. As a result, God trusted Moses with his Word. He trusted this faithful servant to deliver his message to the Israelite people from Mount Sinai. After forty days of intimate contact with the Lord, Moses came down from the Mount with what may be the most important message to the people: the Ten Commandments.

Did Moses have shortcomings? Of course he did. For one thing, he could lose his temper with the people for their grumbling and disobedience. One such episode, in which he struck a rock to get water for the people instead of speaking to it as God commanded, led to him not being allowed to enter the Promised Land (see Numbers 20). But regardless of his shortcomings, God used Moses to bring the Hebrew people together as a nation and unite them under his laws. Furthermore, as we will explore in this session, God used the life of Moses—from birth to death—to reveal the mysteries of the coming Messiah.

SHARE

Before you watch the video teaching, pair up with another member and briefly discuss the following questions:

- Moses was an effective leader for the Israelites. Who would you consider to be an effective leader in your life? What traits does that person possess?

- One of the most important events in Moses' life was his encounter with God at the burning bush (see Exodus 3). When have you experienced this kind of life-changing encounter with God? What new direction did your life take?

WATCH

Watch the video for session four. (Play the DVD or see the instructions on the inside front cover on how to access the sessions through streaming.) As you watch, use the following outline to record any thoughts or concepts that stand out to you.

According to Jewish tradition, when Moses was born, "the whole house in its entirety was filled with light." This was the divine light—the same light that shone on the first day of Creation. The light that radiated from Moses was a sign that the night of exile was coming to an end. The darkness was going to give way to the light of redemption and salvation.

The birth of Moses was meant to be a sneak preview of the birth of the Messiah. When the Messiah was born, the light of God's glory shone just like it shone at Moses' birth. Furthermore, the Magi followed a star (to find the Messiah) that was no ordinary star. It was the light of God's presence that led the wise men to the home of Jesus in Bethlehem.

Jesus said, "I am the light of the world" (John 8:12). Later on, he demonstrated this truth when he went up on the Mount of Transfiguration. He had a few of his disciples with him, and there was Elijah and Moses, standing in their midst. Again, we see the connection to Moses.

When God called Moses, he appeared to him in a burning thornbush (Hebrew *hasineh*). God was saying to the children of Israel, "I feel your pain, and I will never leave you nor forsake you." It was a promise that God was going to do a great work of redemption. Thorns connect to the greater exodus that would come through the Messiah. One of the reasons Jesus had a crown of thorns on the cross was that it connects back to God appearing to Moses in the thornbush.

God told Moses to take off his sandals (Hebrew *na-a-laim*), because he was standing on holy ground. The reason you wear shoes is to protect your feet from the pebbles and jagged things you might step on. Shoes are a physical barrier—but also represent *disconnection*. God told Moses to take off his shoes because he wanted Moses to be completely connected to him.

Two distinctions made Moses unique as a prophet. The first is that God spoke to him *face to face*. God directly communicated to Moses like a man speaks to a friend. This is significant because in the New Testament, we see that Yeshua had an even greater intimacy with God. As we read in John 1:1, Messiah was with God in the beginning, face-to-face with God.

Second, no other prophet performed as many amazing miracles as did Moses. The miracles demonstrate his unique relationship with God and reveal that he had been sent to be the redeemer of Israel. In the New Testament, we also find Jesus performing unique miracles. These miracles closely parallel the miracles that Moses performed in Egypt:

Moses	Jesus
water into blood (Exodus 4:9)	water into wine (John 2:1–11)
manna in the desert (Exodus 16)	multiplies bread and fish (John 6:1–15)
parts the Red Sea (Exodus 14:21)	walks on water (John 6:16–21)

All the miracles that John records reveal that Jesus is the greater than Moses, who brings about a greater redemption, and who causes the miraculous and supernatural to break into our lives. Jesus' miracles and his relationship with God show that he is the greater prophet than Moses.

The first time Moses went to Pharaoh, he took his staff, threw it down, and it became a serpent that swallowed up the staffs of the Egyptian magicians (which had also become serpents). The word for "serpent" in Hebrew is *nachash* and has a numerical value of 358:

358 = serpent (*nachash*)
358 = Messiah (*Mashiach*)

The Messiah, who symbolizes life, will swallow up death, represented by the Egyptian serpent.

One of the things that endeared Moses to the Lord was that he was the humblest man in all of the earth. Moses was so humble that he didn't even want to write in Leviticus 1:1 that the Lord had called him directly. Humility is making yourself small in the sight of God, smaller in the sight of others, and smaller in your own sight. Moses embodied this trait.

Humility is the way to greatness in God's kingdom. It's about making yourself small so that God can be great. You can't be full of yourself and have room for relationship and service to others. If you want to be a great leader—if you want to be like Messiah and like Moses, who embodied humility—you have to humble yourself in the sight of the Lord.

DISCUSS

Now it's your turn. Take a few minutes in your group to discuss what you just watched. Use the following questions to jump-start your discussion, and make sure to read the Scripture passages. Be open to receive what God is teaching you and doing in your group.

1. Moses' story has tremendous application to our lives today as followers of Christ. What topic or mystery or the Messiah in this lesson stood out to you?

2. Read Genesis 1:1–4, Psalm 27:1, Matthew 2:9, Luke 2:9, and John 8:12. *Light* is a significant part of the Bible. God brought light to Creation, Moses, and Jesus. Light has many spiritual meanings. For example, to the shepherds, the light of glory shone just as it did when Moses was born.

What are some other spiritual significances of light? How does knowing Jesus is the light of the world impact you?

3. Read Exodus 3:1–2. God was speaking to Moses from a burning thornbush and calling him to redeem the children of Israel. What is the significance of God speaking through a *thorn*bush? What was God saying to Moses and the children of Israel?

4. Read Exodus 3:5. When God appeared to Moses in the burning bush, one of the things he told him was to take off his sandals, because he was standing on holy ground. What do sandals represent? Given this, why did God want Moses to remove them?

5. Read Deuteronomy 18:18, 34:10–12, and John 1:1. When read together, these two passages unlock one of the most important reasons the Torah (the first five books of the Bible) was written. What was that reason? In what ways was Messiah a prophet like Moses? In what ways was he different?

6. Read Numbers 12:3, 6–8, Matthew 20:28, and John 5:41. According to Numbers, one of the things that endeared Moses to the Lord was that Moses was the humblest man in all of the earth. How did Jesus exemplify Moses-like humility? Why do you think humility is the way to greatness in God's kingdom?

RESPOND

Briefly review the outline for the session four teaching and any notes you took. In the space below, write down the most significant point you took away from this session.

PRAY

Close by praying aloud together for a few minutes, asking God to work in each person's heart as you reflect on the content of this session. Write down any specific prayer requests from your group members in the space below so you can continue praying throughout the week.

M oses, though born a Hebrew, is raised in the court of Pharaoh. As an adult, he witnesses an Egyptian beating a fellow Hebrew, kills the man, and hides his body in the sand. Here is Moses, a man raised in the palace, taking matters into his own hands. He wanted to fix things right now, in his way. As A. W. Pink notes, "Moses was in too big a hurry. He was running before the Lord. God's time had not yet come to deliver Israel. Another forty years must yet run their weary course. But Moses waxed impatient and acted in the energy of the flesh."[4]

As we continue to read Moses' story, we find that he was ultimately called the greatest prophet of Israel (see Deuteronomy 34:10–12). He led the people out of slavery. He wrote the first five books of the Old Testament. Perhaps more than any other figure in the Old Testament, the life of Moses is a powerful portrait that points to the life and work of the Messiah. While Abraham is Israel's *ancestor*, many consider Moses the one who established Israel as a *nation*.

So, how did Moses become Israel's greatest prophet? Since there's always more, we will go deeper in this study to learn more about Moses and God's calling on his life. We will examine the process through which God led him—from shepherd, to leader, to mediator—to ultimately become Israel's greatest prophet. Along the way, we will see that while most of us won't have "burning bush" encounters with God like Moses experienced, the Lord will still call each of us to fulfill the unique destiny that he has prepared for us.

STEPPING OUT AHEAD OF GOD

The day after Moses killed the Egyptian, he encountered two Hebrews arguing and fighting with one another. Moses asked one of the men, "Why are you beating your companion?" (Exodus 2:13). The man answered, "Who made you a ruler and a judge over us? Are you saying you're going to kill me—just as you killed the Egyptian?" (verse 14). Moses, certain his deed had become known, exchanged the palace in Egypt for shepherding in Midian. His eye was not on God, but on man. Moses tried to step ahead of God, but the Lord wasn't ready yet to free the children of Israel. His perfect timetable was in place but, for a while, it was on pause.

1. Read Acts 7:25 and Exodus 13:3. Moses acted impetuously. His motives were sincere, and he showed compassion, yet he acted out of anger instead of obeying God and waiting for his leading. It is hard to believe that the man who would be called the meekest man on earth (see Numbers 12:3) could ever act like this. What do you think God was

teaching Moses as he tended sheep in Midian? What was he revealing to Moses about his timing?

2. Read Proverbs 16:9 and 21:5. In most cases, we don't deliberately jump ahead of God. We make decisions quickly that please us in the moment without thinking of the consequences we may face in the future. What are the factors that cause *you* to step ahead of God?

3. Read Genesis 16:1–6 and Hebrews 11:1–11. God had promised to make Abraham into a great nation, but Sarah was tired of waiting. She distrusted what God had promised and, out of disobedience, caused tremendous consequences that still reverberate today. When was a time you were at this point in your walk with God, trying to figure things out ahead of his schedule?

4. Sarah still appears in the "Hall of Faith." Despite her impatience and insubordination, God fulfilled his promise to her and Abraham twenty-four years later. Despite Sarah's moment of failure, God was faithful to her and to his promise. When was a time that you witnessed God's faithfulness in spite of your actions to circumvent his path?

5. Warren Wiersbe wrote, "God never exalts anyone until that person is ready for it. First the cross, then the crown; first the suffering, then the glory. Moses was under God's hand for forty years before God sent him to deliver the Jews from Egypt."[5] God used Moses' time in the desert to cultivate his character and shape him into the leader he would become. In the process, Moses learned humility—and eventually served as a model of humility to others. What are some ways you can likewise cultivate more humility in your life? In what ways is God calling you to surrender more to his timing instead of trying to do things your own way?

STEPPING OUT WITH GOD

"Significantly, the turning point came in Moses' life when he saw, in the desert, that mysterious burning bush, which flamed and blazed away but, for all the crackling of the fire, was not consumed."[6] Moses was tending sheep near Mount Horeb when he saw the bush on fire. Typically, a thornbush in the desert would be consumed quickly, but this bush continued burning. When Moses approached it, the Lord called out to him, saying, "I am the God of your father, the God of Abraham, Isaac and Jacob" (Exodus 3:6). Moses' life was forever changed. He ultimately stepped out in faith to do what God wanted him to do—in his perfect timing.

6. Read Exodus 3:1–4. When Moses walked over to the bush, God "saw that he turned to look." Moses was open to an interruption in his routine. He could have just passed by, but he didn't. Instead, he stopped and took the time to listen. Many of us today wonder why we don't hear more from God. Maybe the answer is due to our activity—we are just too busy to take the time to listen for God. Is there a "burning bush" in your desert? How could you find some time today to quiet yourself and be open to what God might be saying to you?

7. Read Exodus 3:5–10. Moses took the time to turn and look at the burning bush, and when he did, God called out his name. God then unfolded his plan for Moses when he said, "Come now, I will send you to Pharaoh, so that you may bring My people *Bnei-Yisrael* out from Egypt" (Exodus 3:10). Why do you think God would use a man like Moses—who had failed—for such an important task? Can you think of others in the Bible whom God used in spite of their past?

8. Review the remainder of this story in Exodus 3:11–4:17. Moses is soon arguing with God and giving him several reasons as to why he is not the best choice to free the children of Israel. As the longer story unfolds, we find Moses to be a competent speaker and leader. He is a man of spiritual power who ends up writing the first five books of the Bible (Torah). The lesson here is that God knows us better than we know ourselves. We just need to bury the baggage that restrains the gifts God has given us to do what he has called us to do. What are some things that hold you back from trusting God to do what he tells you to do, in his way?

9. Read Matthew 4:18–19. David Platt wrote, "Jesus' call to the fishermen seems obvious in that context: they dropped their nets and followed Him. They physically walked around with Him wherever He went. And after Jesus' death and resurrection, they followed Him by his way of life and spreading the good news about what He had accomplished in His time on earth. But what does it mean to follow Jesus today?"[7] When was a time that you, like Moses and the disciples, dropped everything you were doing to follow God? How does it help you to trust and obey God when you know you're not alone—when you know there are others on this journey?

WHAT FOLLOWING GOD'S TIMING MEANS FOR YOU

God's vision is key to living the abundant life that Jesus promises in John 10:10. We need to see who we are—our identity in Christ—as well as God's purpose, calling, and mission for our lives from his divine perspective. As we have seen, Moses needed to experience his own *personal* breakthrough before he could help the Israelites experience their *corporate* breakthrough to freedom. God needed to transform Moses' identity so Moses could step into his destiny.

Often, it is our destiny that transforms our identity. Moses went from being a shepherd of sheep to a shepherd of

Israel. This was God's prophetic vision for him. The disciples of Jesus experienced a similar transformation, going from fishermen to fishers of men. God used who the disciples *were* and *where they came from* to make them into *what they were destined to be.* It just required both Moses and the disciples to be obedient to step into God's calling.

10. Read Song of Solomon 1:2 and John 10:27. Mouth-to-mouth, in this context ("the kisses of his mouth"), is understood as God revealing deep truth and revelation to his beloved. It implies intimate communication with God—the type of communication that Jesus and Moses received. A first step in obeying God is listening so you can hear his voice. But what's the next step you must take? (Think about what Moses did when God called him from the burning bush.)

11. Read Exodus 4:9 and John 2:1–11. In the first plague, Moses turned water into blood. In Jesus' first miracle, he turned water not into blood—but into new, sweet wine. Moses' miracle brought death, but Yeshua's miracle brought life. Notice that Jesus' miracle didn't happen until the wine ran out. Many times, when we experience a similar situation, we respond with worry and anxiety. We run around wringing our hands, wondering what we need to do to solve whatever we are facing. But instead, we need to react like Mary, moving from fear, worry, and anxiety to faith. As we

believe, we move from faith to trust that God will show up in his time. When was a time when God showed up just at the right time? How does remembering those kinds of experiences help you stay in step with God's timing?

12. Read Hebrews 3:2–3. Jesus, as the greater than Moses, did all the Father asked him to do. Likewise, Moses remained faithful to tending God's house—meaning the children of Israel. If you want to live the abundant life, you must be willing to be transformed by God, rather than merely living the ordinary life on the backside of Midian. You must take risks obediently and move into what God is calling you to do. Obedience to God's Word, his Will, and his ways are critical components to stepping out in his timing. Contrast the time when Moses was outside of God's timing and, then, inside it. How was he different? How can you likewise be more "faithful to the One who appointed you" as you wait for God's timing in all things?

13. Read Numbers 13:25–33, Matthew 21:21, and Acts 2:14–41. The mind works like a projector. It takes images and magnifies them. You can either magnify why you can't fulfill what God has given you to do (as the ten spies did), or you can magnify the Lord and his promises to you (as Joshua, Caleb, and Peter did). You have a choice to make when it comes to trusting in God—and when you choose to trust in God, you need to then *act* on that faith. What are Jesus' words to those who lack the faith to act? As you listen to God in the coming weeks, will you be open to acting on what he says and not merely listening? Why or why not?

For Next Week: In the next session, you will explore the mysteries of the Messiah as told in the love story of Ruth and Boaz. Before your group gathers, read chapter 11 in *Mysteries of the Messiah*. Also take a few minutes to acquaint or reacquaint yourself with these two important figures from the Old Testament by reviewing Ruth 1–4.

Notes

1. Anthony T. Selvaggio, *From Bondage to Liberty: The Gospel According to Moses*, ed. Iain M. Duguid, The Gospel According to the Old Testament (Phillipsburg, NJ: P&R Publishing, 2014), 32.
2. James Merritt, *Nine Keys to Successful Leadership: How to Impact and Influence Others* (Eugene OR: Harvest House Publishers, 2011), 8.
3. John Maxwell, *The 21 Irrefutable Laws of Leadership* (Nashville, TN: Thomas Nelson, 1998).
4. Arthur Walkington Pink, *Gleanings in Exodus* (Chicago: Moody Press, 1962), 20.
5. Warren W. Wiersbe, *The Bible Exposition Commentary,* vol. 2 (Wheaton, IL: Victor Books, 1996), 432.
6. John Philips, *Exploring Revelation,* rev. ed. (Chicago: Moody, 1987; reprint, Neptune, N.J.: Loizeaux, 1991), 156
7. David Platt, *What Did Jesus Really Mean When He Said Follow Me?* (Wheaton, IL: Tyndale House Publishers, 2013), 1.

FINDING JESUS IN THE STORY OF RUTH AND BOAZ

*In the genealogy of Jesus in Matthew's Gospel,
we find the names of four women: Tamar, Rahab,
Bathsheba, and Ruth. All of these women are Gentiles.
They are from people groups outside of Israel—
and thus outside God's covenantal promise to
Abraham. With the joining of Ruth and Boaz, we find
a restoration between these groups. Boaz and Ruth,
Jew and Gentile, come together to ultimately birth
the messianic line of David. Their story reveals
that we cannot be perfected in unity unless—
like Ruth and Boaz—we are one relationally.*

WELCOME

Many sections of the Bible are devoted to lists of family trees known as *genealogies*. In the Old Testament, we find them in the first five books of the Bible (the books of Moses or Penta-teuch), Ruth, Chronicles, Ezra, and Nehemiah. Often, they are referred to as "the Book of Genealogies" (see Genesis 5:1) or introduced as "these are the genealogical records" (see Genesis 2:4). These biblical genealogies were not merely concerned with biological connections but often focused on occupa-tions (see Genesis 4:17–22) or legitimacy, royal or otherwise.

Most of us tend to skip over these genealogies in our daily study of the Bible. We feel it is a waste of time to read through names we can't pronounce and don't know histori-cally. However, despite how challenging these genealogies may be, they are important for at least two reasons. As Ray Stedman notes: (1) genealogies are important for obtaining a full understanding of the history of Israel, and (2) they are carefully selected and constructed to show God's plan in working through human beings to achieve his purposes.[1] Remember, God put every word in the Bible for a *reason* . . . including the genealogies.

Perhaps the most important genealogies in the Bible are found in the Gospels of Matthew and Luke. We find some differences in the accounts, but one name stands out in each: "*David*, the son of Jesse, the son of Obed, the son of Boaz" (Luke 3:31–32, emphasis added; see also Matthew 1:5–6). As scholars note, "Matthew gives the legal descent of heirship to the throne of *David*, through Joseph, while Luke gives the physical descent of Jesus through Mary. Matthew is concerned with the kingship of Jesus, Luke with his humanity."[2]

The Messiah came through the line of the patriarchs—through Abraham, Isaac, and Jacob—and descended through "David the king" (Matthew 1:6). As Paul wrote, "Concerning His Son, He came into being from the seed of David according to the flesh. He was appointed *Ben-Elohim* [Son of God] in power according to the *Ruach* [Spirit] of holiness, by the resurrection from the dead. He is Messiah *Yeshua* our Lord" (Romans 1:3–4).

Significantly, the genealogies of the Messiah reveal that the grandparents of King David were Boaz and Ruth. Boaz was an Israelite. But Ruth was a *Moabite*—a people group outside of the covenantal promise of God to Abraham. Even so, God saw it fit that his Son—Yeshua, the Messiah—would descend through this union. As we will see in this session, the relationship between Ruth and Boaz reveals much about the mysteries of the Messiah . . . and has implications for followers of Christ even to this day.

SHARE

Before you watch the video teaching, pair up with another member and briefly discuss the following questions:

- Who are some of the key individuals who stand out in your family's genealogy? What contributions did they make that are noteworthy?

- What do you know about the nationalities of the people in your family tree? What mixing between races and cultures do you find in your own family?

WATCH

Watch the video for session five. (Play the DVD or see the instructions on the inside front cover on how to access the sessions through streaming.) As you watch, use the following outline to record any thoughts or concepts that stand out to you.

Ruth and Boaz play a significant role in the promise of the messianic King. The story begins with a couple named Naomi and Elimelech, who settle in Moab—a land cursed by God—during a time of famine. One of their sons marries a Moabite woman named Ruth. When Naomi's husband and two sons die sometime later, she makes the decision to return to Bethlehem.

Ruth makes the decision that she cannot break her connection and relationship with Naomi. She vows to go where Naomi goes—that her people will be her people, and Naomi's God will be her God. Nothing will separate them other than death. Ruth travels to Bethlehem, meets a man named Boaz, and eventually marries him. Their union establishes the genealogy of David.

The coming together of Ruth and Boaz represents the restoration of the relationship between Abraham and Lot. The two had separated when the land could no longer sustain what Abraham and Lot had acquired in one space. Lot went to Sodom and Gomorrah—a place of wickedness. When God judges those cities, Lot and his family are spared.

Lot's daughters believe the end of the world has come and sleep with their father. Two nations are born from those daughters. One of those nations is Moab, which in Hebrew literally means "from my father." Ruth was a descendant of that incestuous relationship. So when Ruth and Boaz come together, it is the restoration of that relationship between Abraham and Lot.

Matthew's genealogy of Jesus is unique in that it lists four women: Tamar, Rahab, Ruth, and Bathsheba. They are all Gentile women. In the same way it took Ruth and Boaz—Jew and Gentile—to birth the messianic line of David, it takes Jew and Gentile to birth the kingdom of God. We cannot be perfected in unity until Jew and Gentile are one relationally.

The rabbis see messianic significance in Ruth 2:14. First, the phrase, "Come over here," speaks prophetically about King David coming from Ruth and Boaz. Sin separates us, but the Messiah—the Son of David—would come to bring God's people near. The Messiah would do this by offering himself as a sacrifice so we could draw near to God.

Boaz says, "Eat some bread." Bread in Jewish thought is associated with the kingdom of God, and especially the Messiah.

We find a connection between *king* and *bread* in the number 90:

90 = bread (*lechem*)
90 = king (*melech*)

Just as Moses gave manna in the wilderness, Jesus gives bread from heaven and multiplies the bread for the people. He is the promised messianic King, the greater than Moses, and the One spoken of in this passage according to the rabbis.

Boaz then says to Ruth, "Dip your piece into the wine vinegar." The rabbis connect this to the suffering of the Messiah in Isaiah 53. We see this being fulfilled in two places in the New Testament. One is at the Last Supper, when Judas dips his piece of bread in the sop.[3] The second is when Jesus was on the cross and was offered wine vinegar. Both of these references point to this verse in Ruth being fulfilled in Jesus, the Messiah.

The number 8 is significant in the book of Ruth because it points to David:

8 = David (eighth son of Jesse)
8 = covenant (circumcise male boys on the eighth day)
8 = supernatural (rises above seven)
8 = resurrection (Jesus rose on eighth day of the week)
8 = new beginnings

In Greek, the name of Jesus adds up to 8, 8, 8. He is the ultimate son of David. He brings the covenant. He is the resurrection. He offers us a new beginning.

The story of Ruth reveals the importance of relationship and connection. Ruth made a commitment to leave everything behind so she could cleave to God and cleave to Naomi. She didn't want to leave the connection. Friendship and connection are critical components of living a life of blessing. God's blessing always happens in the context of relationship.

God doesn't want you to live out of lack. He wants you to live out of the overflow. But abundant life comes through abundant relationships. So let's be true friends of the Lord and true friends of those whom he places in our lives. Jesus came and died so that we might have friendship with God. He calls us friends if we follow him and believe in him.

DISCUSS

Now it's your turn. Take a few minutes in your group to discuss what you just watched. Use the following questions to jump-start your discussion, and make sure to read the Scripture passages. Be open to receive what God is teaching you and doing in your group.

1. Boaz and Ruth's love story has many applications for us today. What topic or mystery in this week's lesson especially stood out to you?

2. Read Genesis 13:5–18, Ruth 1:1–4, and 1 Peter 5:10. Ruth was a Moabite, a descendant of the incestuous relationship between Lot and his daughter. When Lot left Abraham, he

ultimately lost everything. But when Ruth and Boaz married, there is a restoration of Abraham and Lot's relationship. Why is this significant?

3. Read Matthew 1:1–17. One of the mysteries of the Messiah is that contained in Jesus' genealogy are the names of four Gentile women. What do you think this is meant to show us about Jesus? What is it meant to teach us?

4. Read Psalm 133 and John 17:20–23. We cannot be perfected in unity until Jew and Gentile are one relationally just as Ruth and Boaz were. The world will not be won, *W-O-N*, until we are one, *O-N-E*, in Jesus . Why is this significant? What are the barriers to unity? What are some ways you can overcome these barriers?

5. Read Ruth 2:14 and Ephesians 2:13. Sin separates us from God and creates a distance from him. The Hebrew word for sacrifice is *korban,* which means to "draw near." The

Messiah is the One who draws us near to the kingdom of God. What is the significance of Boaz asking Ruth to "come over here"? How does drawing near to God create an intimacy with him that helps us to live the abundant life that he offers?

6. As discussed in this week's teaching, there are two types of relationships: contractual and covenantal. How would you define each type of relationships? What type of relationship did Ruth and Boaz have? How do these types of relationships lead to abundant life in the family of God?

RESPOND

Briefly review the outline for the session five teaching and any notes you took. In the space below, write down the most significant point you took away from this session.

PRAY

Close by praying aloud together for a few minutes, asking God to work in each person's heart as you reflect on the content of this session. Write down any specific prayer requests from your group members in the space below so you can continue praying throughout the week.

BETWEEN-SESSIONS PERSONAL STUDY

As you have heard me say throughout this study . . . *there is always more*. Remember, everything in Scripture was written for the sake of the Messiah, and the book of Ruth is no exception. As we discussed this week, the Jewish rabbis examined parts of the story of Ruth and the ways those sections applied it to the Messiah. For this week's personal study, you are going to go deeper into those connections. Begin by reading Ruth 2:14 slowly, engaging every word. This one verse reveals many important mysteries of the Messiah.

COME AND EAT

In Ruth 2, we find the incredible generosity of Boaz. He shows hospitality to a foreigner (remember that Ruth was from Moab). He calls her by a warm word and invites her to eat with him. But something deeper is implied by Boaz's dialogue with Ruth. As Jesus states, "You search the Scriptures because you suppose that in them you have eternal life. It is these that testify about Me" (John 5:39). All the Scriptures testify about Jesus. So when Boaz says to Ruth, "Come over here," he is alluding, on a prophetic level, to Ruth's future descendant, Messiah, who would establish the messianic Kingdom. The phrase "coming near" is important in Jewish thought. It has been interpreted by the rabbis as "come/draw near to the Kingdom."[4]

1. Read Ephesians 2:13–17, John 7:37, and Mark 10:14. Jesus' primary mission was to enable us to draw near to God. What does it mean to you that Jesus is inviting you to "come over here"?

2. Max Lucado notes, "[God's] invitation is for life. An invitation to come into his kingdom and take up residence in a tearless, graveless, painless world."[5] How is your faith strengthened by Jesus' invitation to come and be part of an eternal community in his eternal presence?

3. Read 1 Corinthians 1:24. Nearness to Jesus means spiritual intimacy. How would you define spiritual intimacy with God? How could you become more spiritually intimate with Jesus?

4. Read Matthew 14:13–21. Boaz's invitation for Ruth to "eat some bread" alludes to "bread in the kingdom of God" (Luke 14:15). The Messiah, like Moses, would provide bread from heaven and would actually be "the bread of life" (John 6:35). Bread was an important part of the first century diet. Jesus, after preaching to the 5,000, says, "They need not go away; you give them something to eat." (Matthew 14:16). In what ways does Jesus give us "something to eat" today? How does the bread of life Jesus provides nourish us?

5. Read Matthew 6:10–11 and James 1:17. Every good thing comes from God, including being part of his kingdom. What does it mean for you to be part of his kingdom?

DIPPING, SITTING, AND PROVIDING

Boaz knew Ruth's story. As he demonstrates grace to her, and invites her to eat with him, he provides us with vital clues about the Messiah. When Jesus came to earth, he sought people to come and feast with him. The Messiah, like Boaz, made every effort to include those on the "outside" and make them feel loved, cared for, and accepted.

Boaz's invitation for Ruth to "dip your piece into the wine vinegar" points to the suffering of the Messiah. As the prophet Isaiah wrote, "He was pierced because of our transgressions, crushed because of our iniquities. The chastisement for our shalom was upon Him, and by His stripes we are healed" (53:5). Ruth's dipping her "piece into the vinegar [sop]" also alludes to the Messiah's death on the cross.

1. Read John 13:18–30. What chain of events begins with the handing of the sop to Judas?

2. Read Luke 22:14–23. Dipping the sop was part of the Last Supper (the Passover Seder). How does dipping the sop remind you of communion and Jesus' death?

3. Ruth received Boaz's invitation and "sat beside the harvesters" (Ruth 2:14). In Jewish thought, this phrase alludes to the kingship being taken from the Messiah for a time. The key question is *when*. In Isaiah 53:3–5, we read that the kingship was taken away when the majority of the Jewish people rejected Jesus as Messiah. The Messiah was rejected and, like Moses, had to be concealed for a time until the day Israel's final redemption comes. Why is it important to know that Jesus is now "hidden," but that he will one day be "revealed" and come again?

4. Read John 6:37. What does it mean to you that "anyone coming to Me I will never reject"? How are you actively extending this invitation to others who need to receive God's grace?

5. Ruth's marriage to Boaz points to the greater fulfillment of grace and the truth in the person of the Messiah. Boaz shows Ruth incredible grace, protection, and provision. Likewise, the Messiah, when we trust fully in him, gives us a vast amount of grace, protection, and provision. The key is looking forward to the promises of the Messiah and what he can do in your life. Paul wrote, "Our God gives you everything you need, makes you everything you're to be" (2 Thessalonians 1:2 MSG). Boaz personally shared his own side dish with Ruth when "held out her roasted grain" (Ruth 2:14). How does this compare to Jesus sharing all that he has with you?

6. Read 2 Timothy 3:16–17, Psalm 119:105, and Matthew 4:4. Ruth is not only invited to come, but also to eat. We are likewise invited to consume God's Word. How do his promises from the Word inspire you? How have they served to nourish you in your life?

WHAT BOAZ AND RUTH'S STORY MEANS FOR YOU

The book of Ruth has several themes. It's a book of redemption. It's a book of survival and loyalty. But it's also a book of mercy and kindness. The Hebrew word translated "kindness" in Ruth is *chesed*. It can be translated as "mercy," "lovingkindness," "steadfast love," and "compassion."[6] *Chesed* is everlasting. It's love in action. It's the love God has for his people. It's a love we need to extend to others. Ruth is full of *chesed*.

7. Read Ruth 1:6–15. Naomi recognizes that God is faithful and loving. She prays for her daughters-in-law that they will experience his *chesed*—his mercy and lovingkindness. What does God's lovingkindness and mercy mean to you? Who could you pray for today, asking God to extend his *chesed* to them?

8. Read Ruth 2:19–23. Naomi's hope is restored after experiencing her difficult circumstances, and she blesses Boaz for his kindness. Boaz goes on to redeem them from their difficulties and lay the foundation of the messianic line of David. What are some situations in your life that have caused you to feel hopeless? How have you witnessed God redeem and restore those times?

9. Read Ruth 3:7–15 and 4:13–21. Boaz could have to take the steps necessary to make Ruth his wife. But he loved her and chose her—just as our Messiah loves us, chooses us, and accepts us. How did Boaz show the kindness (*chesed*)

of the kinsman redeemer? How does knowing that God loves you, chooses you, and accepts you after the way you feel about yourself?

10. Read John 1:14–17. Jesus was "full of grace." This suggests *chesed* as a part of Yeshua's character. As William Barclay wrote, "The fact that God came to earth to live and to die for men and women is not something which humanity deserved; it is an act of pure love on the part of God. The word "grace" emphasizes at one and the same time our own helpless poverty and God's limitless kindness."[7] Contrast the kindness of Boaz (who he was, how he treated Ruth, what he did for Ruth) with the kindness you find in Jesus. What are some of the ways you see Jesus' *chesed* in your life? In what ways can you reflect his mercy and lovingkindness to others?

For Next Week: In the final session, you will explore the mysteries of the Messiah as revealed in the story of David. Before your group gathers, read chapter 12 in *Mysteries of the Messiah*. Also take a few minutes to acquaint or reacquaint yourself with David's early life, anointing, and adversity faced at the hands of King Saul by reviewing 1 Samuel 16–19.

Notes

1. Ray C. Stedman, *Adventuring Through the Bible: Old Testament* (Grand Rapids, MI: Discovery House Publishers, 2011), eBook edition.
2. J. D. Douglas, Merrill C. Tenney, Moisés Silva, *Zondervan Illustrated Bible Dictionary* (Grand Rapids, MI: Zondervan, 2011), 515.
3. A sop is "a think piece of bread, dipped into a common dish and used as a spoon (John 13:26)." Walter Elwell, General Editor, Baker Encyclopedia of the Bible, (Grand Rapids, MI: Baker Book House, 1988), 1985.
4. *Midrash Rabbah: The Five Megillos—Ruth*, vol. 1, Kleinman ed. (Brooklyn, NY: Mesorah Publications, 2013), 49:1.
5. Max Lucado, *Everyday Blessings: Inspirational Thoughts from the Published Works of Max Lucado* (Nashville, TN: Thomas Nelson, Inc., 2004), Logos Software Edition.
6. "Putting the *Chesed* of Adonai Before Your Eyes," Hebrew4Christians, https://hebrew4christians.com/Meditations/Chesed/chesed.html
7. William Barclay, *The Gospel of John,* Rev. and updated., vol. 1, *The New Daily Study Bible* (Edinburgh: Saint Andrew Press, 2001), 77.

FINDING JESUS IN THE STORY OF DAVID

The Bible reveals the Messiah was present with God at the time of Creation. He was to come through the line of the patriarchs—through Abraham, Isaac, and Jacob. He was to be both a suffering servant and reigning king who would come to bring redemption and restoration between humans and God. He would be the greater than Moses. These are just some of the "mysteries of the Messiah" found in Scripture. But there's more! David's life and lineage provide even further insights and revelation into the person and work of the Messiah. The promised Son of David would be so much more than just a biological descendant of David's lineage.

WELCOME

David is a beloved figure in Scripture. He was God's anointed king, and it was from his line the promised Messiah was to come. As the Lord declared to him, "ADONAI will make a house for you. When your days are done and you sleep with your fathers, I will raise up your seed, who will come forth from you after you, and I will establish his kingdom. He will build a house for My Name, and I will establish his royal throne forever" (2 Samuel 7:11–13).

Why did God chose David for this role? The answer is clear: "ADONAI has sought for Himself a man after His own heart. So ADONAI will appoint him as ruler over His people" (1 Samuel 13:14). David was a man who *sought after God's own heart* and trusted in him. As a result, "David had success in all his undertakings, since [the Lord] was with him" (18:14).

The Hebrew word translated "success" in this verse is *sākal*. It means "to be wise, understand, prosper/be success-ful."[1] This was sadly not true of Israel's current king, a man named Saul. "Now Saul became afraid of David, because ADONAI was with him but had departed from Saul. Therefore Saul removed him from his entourage by appointing him as a captain of a thousand. So David went out and came in before the troops" (verses 12–13).

Saul was afraid of David. "He dreaded him" (verse 15). In fact, we read that Saul went so far as to throw a spear at David in an attempt to end his life (see verse 11). But David acted wisely. He fled from King Saul's presence and, rather than immediately staging a rebellion, chose to wait and trust in God's timing. Saul may have had physical skill when it came to tossing spears, but David had spiritual wisdom. Whether fighting giants, dodging projectiles, or leading armies, David's trust in God led him to a unique spiritual wisdom.

David's spiritual wisdom must have been obvious to the people for *all* of Israel and Judah to love him. What's more, David didn't use his popularity to overthrow Saul. He didn't allow his fame to lead to a swelled head. While Saul allowed his relationship with God to steadily sink, David committed to keeping his relationship on the rise. As a result, David was given success (*s kal*) in all his undertakings.

The apostle Paul wrote to Timothy, "Do not neglect the spiritual gift within you, which was given to you through prophecy with the laying on of hands of the elders. Practice these things—be absorbed in them, so that your progress may be clear to all. Give attention to yourself and your teaching. Persevere in these things, for in doing so you will save yourself and those who hear you" (1 Timothy 4:14-18).

David demonstrated such perseverance. Everything about his life points to the hand of God. He was truly "a man after [God's] heart" (Acts 13:22). And, as we will discover in this final session, his life has much to reveal about the person and work of the Messiah.

SHARE

Before you watch the video teaching, pair up with another member and briefly discuss the following questions:

- Both David *and* Saul were anointed by God to serve as kings of Israel. Why do you think David had greater success in this role?

- What does it mean to you to have spiritual wisdom? How would you describe the difference between worldly wisdom and wisdom that comes from God?

WATCH

Watch the video for session six. (Play the DVD or see the instructions on the inside front cover on how to access the sessions through streaming.) As you watch, use the following outline to record any thoughts or concepts that stand out to you.

David is a key figure and a beloved individual in the Bible. In Hebrew, his name has three consonants: *dalet*, *vav*, *dalet*. The middle letter of David's name is the *vav*—the letter of connection. David was a man after God's own heart because he sought intimate connection with the Lord. We see this in the meaning of David's name: "beloved."

How did David seek that connection? He loved the Word of the Lord. He meditated on it day and night. He delighted in it. The Word of God—the *vav*—was at the center of his life.

Vav is the sixth letter in the Hebrew alphabet. We find other connections between the number 6, David, and the Word of God:

6 = day on which David was born (sixth day of Sivan)
6 = day on which David died (sixth day of Sivan)
6 = Day of Pentecost (the giving of God's Word)

David was connected to the Word of God. It was at the center of his life. It needs to be at the center of our lives if we want that deeper connection to the Lord as well.

The Holy Spirit was poured out on the people on the Day of Pentecost. Word and Spirit came on the exact same day. In the book of Genesis, we read how Creation came by the Word of God. The Spirit of God was hovering over the deep, and God spoke Creation into existence. In the same way, *new* creation comes by Word and Spirit. David was a man who pursued both.

Jesus was the greater than Moses, but he was also the greater than David. When God called Moses, he was shepherding the sheep. When God called David, he was also serving his family as a shepherd. David and Moses, as shepherds, prophetically point to Jesus, who said, "I am the Good Shepherd" (John 10:11). Jesus is willing to lay down his life for the sheep.

Jesus was born in Bethlehem, the same location where David was born and learned to become a shepherd. Jesus is the royal king from the family of David, born in Bethlehem to be a shepherd. He is the ultimate shepherd. Everything in David's life as a shepherd, and in Moses' life as a shepherd, points to Jesus and finds its fulfillment in him.

David, in Hebrew, has a numerical value of 14 (*dalet* = 4, *vav* = 6, *dalet* = 4). In Matthew's genealogy, he breaks up the generations in groups of 14:

14 = generations between Abraham and David
14 = generations between David and the Exile
14 = generations between the Exile and the Messiah

Matthew is spelling out the name of David, saying that all the generations find their fulfillment in the birth of Jesus. He is the promised Seed of the woman.

One of the gifts the wise men bring to Jesus is gold. In Hebrew, the word is *zahav,* and it has a numerical value of 14. So, the wise men come to worship the Son of David, born in the city of David, and bring him gold in recognition of his royalty. All of these are connected to the number 14. It's as if they are saying, "Jesus, you are truly the King of Israel sent by God."

The number 14 is associated with redemption. The way you write 14 in Hebrew literally means "hand." God redeemed Israel through Moses at the Passover. The Passover was to begin on the 14th day of the month of Nisan—the day the lamb was slaughtered.

The Passover had to begin on the 14th day because God brought Israel out of Egypt with a mighty hand (*yad hazakah*) and an outstretched arm (*zeroa netuyah*). When Jesus gives his life on the cross, he dies on the 14th day of the month of Nisan, because it is the hand of God working redemption through Christ. He is God's hand revealed in history to redeem us.

The two hands of God connect to the two comings of the Messiah. God's hand was revealed in Jesus' first coming. People couldn't recognize him and didn't understand who he was. But at the second coming, he will fully be revealed. He will defeat the enemies of God and establish his kingdom on earth as it is in heaven. May that day come speedily and soon!

Just as David was God's beloved, you have become his number one kid. His number one son or his number one daughter. Identity is destiny. Know that you are beloved in him. This will give you hope and will allow you to do great things for him, both now and in the future.

DISCUSS

Now it's your turn. Take a few minutes in your group to discuss what you just watched. Use the following questions to jump-start your discussion, and make sure to read the Scripture passages. Be open to receive what God is teaching you and doing in your group.

1. What part of Rabbi Jason's teaching stood out to you in this session as it relates to the mysteries of the Messiah as revealed in the story of King David?

2. David's name consists of three Hebrew letters: *dalet, vav, dalet. Vav* in Hebrew is the letter of connection. *Vav* and connection point to the essence of who David was at his core. How did David foster that deep connection to God? What must be at the center of your heart and life if you want a similar deep connection with the Lord?

3. Read Psalm 51:12–13, John 3:5, and Ephesians 1:17–20. Besides God's Word, what is foundational to have an

intimate connection with God? What are the blessings of pursuing God's Word and the Spirit in your life?

4. Read Ezekiel 34:23, John 10:11–17, and Matthew 2:6. Moses and David were great shepherds, but they didn't compare to Jesus. How does Jesus describe his role as our "Good Shepherd"? What does he promise to do for his "sheep"?

5. Read Isaiah 53:1 and 63:5. God rescued the children of Israel from Egyptian bondage by his mighty hand. When Jesus died on the cross, it represented the hand of God bringing redemption through Jesus. How has God's hand redeemed and rescued you?

6. Read Psalm 39:8, 42:6, and Romans 8:28. Sometimes you can see God's hand at work, while other times his actions will be hidden from you. David learned to accept God's hand in all things. What kind of faith do you need to do the same? How has God's hidden hand worked out "all things for good" in any challenge you have faced?

RESPOND

Briefly review the outline for the session six teaching and any notes you took. In the space below, write down the most significant point you took away from this session.

PRAY

Close by praying aloud together for a few minutes, asking God to work in each person's heart as you reflect on the content of this session. Write down any specific prayer requests from your group members in the space below so you can continue praying throughout the week.

FINAL PERSONAL STUDY

In this session, we have examined David from many perspectives. As we continue to study this hero and forerunner of the Messiah, we cannot forget that he was also a songwriter who wrote so many beautiful psalms that appear in the Bible. Many of these psalms of David allude to the Messiah. In this final personal study, you will explore some of these connections between the Davidic Psalms and the hopes for a future victorious Messiah.

DAVID, THE KINGLY PROPHET

The rabbis tell us that David was the greatest Torah scholar of his generation.[2] Therefore, it only makes sense that David's study would lead him to know and write psalms about the Messiah. The Holy Spirit inspired David to write most of these psalms, the worship manual of Israel, and he prophetically spoke of Messiah in many of them. David certainly wrote about his own experiences. But underlying his writing, the focus was not on himself as king, but on the King of kings. As one author said, "The agony of the cross was not something David could have witnessed. The resurrection was not something he could have thought of. Yet, he identified closely with the Christ [Messiah] and wrote things as the Spirit of God revealed them."[3]

1. Read Psalm 2, Hebrews 1:5, and Revelation 11:15. In Psalm 2, David clearly described the Messiah. What names can you find in that psalm that relate to Yeshua? What does David predict?

2. Read Psalm 16. The opening verse states this is a miktam (or michtam) psalm of David. "Some translate the word 'golden,' i.e., precious. The root of the word means to stamp or grave, and hence it is regarded as denoting a composition so precious as to be worthy to be engraven on a durable tablet for preservation; or, as others render, 'a psalm precious as stamped gold,' from the word *kethem*, fine or stamped gold.' "[4] David wrote this psalm during a time of crisis, but it also powerfully speaks of the Messiah. What can you find in this psalm that describes Messiah? What can you find that describes what the Messiah does for us?

3. Read Psalm 22 and Matthew 27:46. This is one of David's finest messianic psalms and one of the most significant prophecies in the Bible. How does this psalm point to Yeshua, the greater David? What can you learn about what Jesus was thinking from David's song?

4. Read Psalm 24 and Psalm 68:18. As one scholar notes, "Psalm 24 will deal with the crown. Psalm 22 deals with Jesus' death and Psalm 23 with His life. . . . Here in Psalm 24, we'll see the Chief Shepherd who is coming back for us (1 Peter 5:4)."[5] Who truly has "clean hands and a pure heart" (Psalm 24:4)? How is your faith strengthened when you consider the "everlasting doors" (verse 9) will open again—that Jesus is coming again?

DAVID, THE SHEPHERD PROPHET

David, a man of passionate worship and prayer, spent many of his days in the field as a shepherd. In Jewish tradition, David's ability to shepherd his father's sheep is one of the primary reasons the Lord selected him to be Israel's royal shepherd. The Lord knew that if David could treat literal sheep as well as he did, he would be able to shepherd God's own people. God's choice of David, the compassionate shepherd, forms the New Testament background for Jesus' statement, "I am the Good Shepherd" (John 10:11).

5. Read Psalm 23, 1 Samuel 16:10–11, John 10:11, Hebrews 13:20, and 1 Peter 5:4. In Psalm 23, we find David describing the Lord as a shepherd. Picture David, in a valley, tending his flock. He looks out, and the Holy Spirit gives him a vision of the Messiah as Master Shepherd. As you read the Psalm, what blessings has the Master Shepherd brought to your life? How has he led you through dark valleys into green pastures?

6. If the Lord is your shepherd, it means you are his sheep. "So you, My sheep, the sheep of My pastures, you are human, and I am your God" (Ezekiel 34:31). What should be your attitude if you are indeed a sheep being led by your shepherd, Jesus?

7. Read Psalm 78:66–72, Luke 15:3–6, John 10:11–18. Shepherding is one of the oldest occupations in the world. David's life as a shepherd continued as he became Israel's king. How would you summarize the life of a shepherd?

8. What must a shepherd do to take care of his flock properly? What characteristics does Jesus, Messiah, have that make him the Master Shepherd?

9. Read Psalm 28 and Matthew 11:28. David wrote this psalm during a difficult time. It is possible he wrote it when facing Goliath, or, as many commentators believe, when his son Absalom led an insurrection against him. Whatever the circumstance, David returns to his roots as a shepherd (see Psalm 28:8–9). Although David is in a tough place, he knows the Good Shepherd is there too. What kind of rest does God offer? When was a time when you felt under attack or weak and you felt the Good Shepherd's presence?

WHAT DAVID'S MESSIANIC PSALMS MEANS FOR YOU

As we look at the messianic psalms of David, it's clear that David wrote them under the inspiration of the Holy Spirit. The Lord led him to take a step away from his own experiences and look ahead to compose these songs about the coming Messiah. When we read them, at one level we find David describing his own trials and tribulations. But at another level, we discover a glimpse of the suffering and victories of God's Son. God is revealing to David a picture of the Messiah approximately 1,000 years before he was born.

The fact that David, Yeshua's ancestor, wrote about him is significant. Yeshua is often referred in Scripture as the Son of David. Here, we have evidence of David looking ahead to the real King, the Good Shepherd, the Redeemer. If David and the other prophets can look forward and clearly see Jesus, then shouldn't we likewise set our hearts and minds on the Messiah?

10. Read Psalm 8, Luke 17:22–33, and Hebrews 2:14–18. In Psalm 8, David speaks of the "son of man" (see Psalm 8:5). This is a name that Jesus applies to himself (see Luke 17:22, 24, 25, 30). What does the phrase "son of man" mean to you? According to the author of Hebrews, what this significance of this title?

11. Read Psalm 31, 2 Samuel 22:1, and Luke 21:28. David writes in Psalm 31 about being protected by God. By the end of the psalm, he is asking God for deliverance and then strongly urging others to depend on God totally. David saw a vision of Yeshua's protection and deliverance in both his first and second comings. How has Jesus protected and delivered you? How will he protect and deliver you eternally?

12. Read Psalm 51 and Romans 5:1–11. David had his difficulties, and at times he sinned. In Psalm 51, we find him seeking redemption. How does David describe himself? What is he asking God to provide? What does Paul say the Messiah did for us in this regard?

13. Read Psalm 40 and Romans 8:1–2. David describes how God brought him "up out of the slimy pit, out of the mud and mire" and "set my feet on a rock" (Psalm 40:3). David finds his hope and peace by placing himself in God's hands, knowing that the Lord will not forsake him in spite of the sins of his past. How does it comfort you to know that Jesus accepts you and welcomes you as you are? How do you respond to the fact that there is "no condemnation for those who are in Messiah Yeshua" (Romans 8:1)?

Notes

1. William D. Mounce, *Mounce's Complete Expository Dictionary of Old & New Testament Words* (Grand Rapids, MI: Zondervan, 2006), 547.
2. "Psalms (Tehilim)," Torah.org, https://torah.org/learning/basics-primer-torah-psalms/.
3. Stephen Watkins, *Jesus Our Jewish Messiah,* vol. 1: Once in Time, (Flagstaff AZ: Lessons from Heaven Publications, LLC, 2009), 32.
4. M. G. Easton, *Easton's Bible Dictionary* (New York: Harper & Brothers, 1893).
5. Jon Courson, *Jon Courson's Application Commentary: Volume Two: Psalms–Malachi* (Nashville, TN: Thomas Nelson, 2006), 30.

LEADER'S GUIDE

Thank you for your willingness to lead your group through this study. What you have chosen to do is valuable and will make a great difference in the lives of others. Small groups are important in God's work. As Howard Snyder wrote, "Virtually every major movement of spiritual renewal in the Christian church has been accompanied by a return to the small group and the proliferation of such groups in private homes for Bible study, prayer and discussion of the faith."[1] Small groups provide tremendous opportunities for intimate fellowship among believers in Christ, prayer, and learning that leads to spiritual growth.

Mysteries of the Messiah is a six-session study built around video content and small-group interaction. As the group leader, your role is not to answer all the questions or reteach the content—the video, book, and study guide will do most of that work. Your job is to guide the experience and cultivate your small group into a kind of teaching community. This will make it a place for members to process, question, and reflect on what they are learning.

Before your first meeting, make sure everyone in the group gets a copy of the study guide. This will keep everyone on the same page and help the process run more smoothly. If some group members are unable to purchase the guide, arrange it so that people can share the resource with other group members. Giving everyone access to all the material will position this study to be as rewarding an experience as possible. Everyone should feel free to write in his or her study guide and bring it to the group every week. Also, make sure the group members are aware that they have access to the videos at any time by following the instructions on the inside front cover.

SETTING UP THE GROUP

You will need to determine with your group how long you want to meet each week so you can plan your time accordingly. Generally, most groups like to meet for either ninety minutes or two hours, so you could use one of the following schedules:

SECTION	90 MINUTES	120 MINUTES
WELCOME (members arrive and get settled)	10 minutes	15 minutes
SHARE (discuss one or more of the opening questions for the session)	15 minutes	20 minutes
WATCH (watch the teaching material together and take notes)	25 minutes	25 minutes
DISCUSS (discuss the Bible study questions you selected ahead of time)	30 minutes	45 minutes
RESPOND / PRAY (reflect on the message, pray together as a group, and dismiss)	10 minutes	15 minutes

As group leader, you will want to create an environment that encourages sharing and learning. A church sanctuary or formal classroom may not be as ideal as a living room, as those locations can feel formal and less intimate. No matter what setting you choose, provide enough comfortable seating for everyone, and, if possible, arrange the seats in a semicircle so everyone can see the video teaching easily. This will make transition between the video and group conversation more efficient and natural.

Also, try to get to the meeting site early so that you can greet participants as they arrive. Simple refreshments create a welcoming atmosphere and can be a wonderful addition to a group study evening. Try to take food and pet allergies into account to make your guests as comfortable as possible. You may also want to consider offering childcare to couples with children who want to attend. Finally, be sure your media technology is working properly. Managing these details up front will make the rest of your group experience flow smoothly and provide a welcoming space in which to engage the content of *Mysteries of the Messiah*.

STARTING THE GROUP TIME

Once everyone has arrived, it's time to begin the group. Here are some simple tips to make your group time healthy, enjoyable, and effective.

First, begin the meeting with a short prayer and remind the group members to put their phones on silent. This is a way to make sure you can all be present with one another and with God. Next, give each person a few minutes to respond to the questions in the "Share" section. This won't require as much time in session one, but beginning in session two, people might need more time to share their insights from their personal studies. Usually, you won't answer the discussion questions yourself, but you can go first with the "Share" questions, answering briefly and with a reasonable amount of transparency.

At the end of session one, invite the group members to complete the between-sessions personal studies for that week and read the corresponding chapters in *Mysteries of the Messiah* for the next group session. Let them know it is not a problem if they can't get to some of the between-sessions activities some weeks. It will still be beneficial for them to hear from the other participants and learn about what they discovered.

LEADING THE DISCUSSION TIME

Now that the group is engaged, watch the video together and then respond with some directed small-group discussion. (Play the DVD or see the instructions on the inside front cover on how to access the sessions through streaming.) Encourage all the members to participate in the discussion. As the discussion progresses, you may want to follow up with comments such as, "Tell me more about that," or, "Why did you answer that way?" This will allow the group participants to deepen their reflections and invite meaningful sharing in a nonthreatening way.

Note that you have been given multiple questions to use in each session, and you do not have to use them all or even follow them in order. Feel free to pick and choose questions based on either the needs of your group or how the conversation is flowing. Also, don't be afraid of silence. Offering a question and allowing up to thirty seconds of silence is okay. It allows people space to think about how they want to respond and also gives them time to do so.

As group leader, you are the boundary keeper for your group. Do not let anyone (yourself included) dominate the group time. Keep an eye out for group members who might be tempted to "attack" folks they disagree with or try to "fix" those having struggles. These kinds of behaviors can derail a group's momentum, so they need to be steered in a different direction. Model active listening and encourage everyone in your group to do the same. This will make your group time a safe space and create a positive community.

The group discussion leads to a closing time of response and reflection. Encourage the members to take a few moments to review what they have learned, as this will help them cement the big ideas in their minds. Conclude by praying together as a group.

GROUP DYNAMICS

Leading a group study can be a rewarding experience for you and your group members—but that doesn't mean there won't be challenges. Certain members may feel uncomfortable discussing topics that they consider personal and might be afraid of being called on. Some members might have disagreements on specific issues. To help prevent these scenarios, consider the following ground rules:

- If someone has a question that may seem off topic, suggest that it is discussed at another time, or ask the group if they are okay with addressing that topic.

- If someone asks a question you don't know the answer to, confess that you don't know and move on. If you feel comfortable, invite other group members to give their opinions or share their comments based on personal experience.

- If you feel like a couple of people are talking much more than others, direct questions to people who may not have shared yet. You could even ask the more dominating members to help draw out the quiet ones.

- When there is a disagreement, encourage the group members to process the matter in love. Invite members from opposing sides to evaluate their opinions and consider the ideas of the other members. Lead the group through Scripture that addresses the topic, and look for common ground.

When issues arise, encourage your group to follow these words from Scripture: "Love one another" (John 13:34), "If possible, so far as it depends on you, live in *shalom* [peace] with all people" (Romans 12:18), "Whatever is true . . . honorable . . . just . . . lovely . . . if there is any virtue and if there is anything worthy of praise—dwell on these things" (Philippians 4:8), and, "Be quick to listen, slow to speak, and slow to anger" (James 1:19). This will make your group time more rewarding and beneficial for everyone who attends.

Thank you again for your willingness to lead your group. May God reward your efforts and dedication, equip you to guide your group in the weeks ahead, and make your time together in *Mysteries of the Messiah* fruitful for his kingdom.

Also available from
RABBI JASON SOBEL

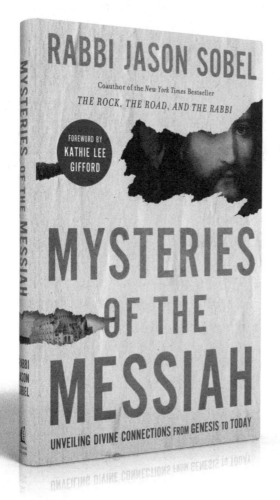

Now available wherever books and ebooks are sold.

For more information, visit
mysteriesofthemessiahbook.com

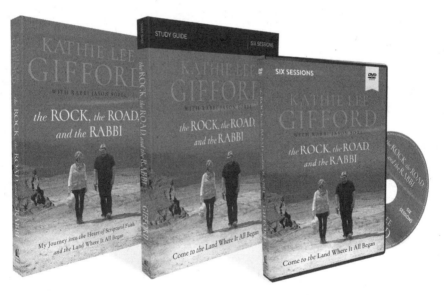